Walk Around

Fw 190D

By E. Brown Ryle and Malcolm Laing
Color by Don Greer
Illustrated by Ernesto Cumpian

Walk Around Number 10

squadron/signal publications

Introduction

The Fw 190D was an in-line engine variant of the radial engine Fw 190. The in-line engine installation was designed to increase the aircraft's performance at altitudes above 24,000 feet where the radial engine did not perform well and the American bomber formations operated.

In May of 1942 the Luftwaffe issued a requirement to Messerschmitt and Focke-Wulf for a 'special high altitude fighter'. Both companies submitted proposals for the new fighter. The proposal submitted by Kurt Tank, the designer of the Fw 190, would result in a much refined Fw 190 — the larger, and longer-winged Ta 152 powered by an in-line engine.

Design and testing of the proposed high altitude fighters did not progress well and the Luftwaffe realized that the needed 'altitude fighter' would not arrive any time soon. In July of 1943 the Luftwaffe requested that both companies find a 'quick solution high altitude fighter'!

In late 1943 Focke-Wulf finalized its 'quick solution'. The Fw 190A-8/9 airframe was strengthened and lengthened to accommodate the longer Junkers Jumo 213A (bomber) engine. The sub-type was designated Fw 190D-9. Prototypes of the new aircraft were tested through out the first half of 1944 with the type being accepted by the Luftwaffe during the early summer of 1944.

Deliveries of Fw 190D-9 to operational units began in August of 1944. First impressions by fighter pilots of the Dora-9, with its bomber engine, were not enthusiastic. Kurt Tank appealed to the pilots by explaining that this aircraft was a temporary fix until the Ta 152 was available.

This less than joyous reaction to the new aircraft's arrival would prove to be the exact opposite of the aircraft's operational career. Once pilots became familiar with the Langnasen-Dora (long-nosed D), they were quite pleased with its performance and capabilities. In the closing months of the war the Fw 190D proved itself a match for any Allied fighter encountered in combat.

Fw 190Ds were built in sub-assemblies by many sub-contractors through out Germany and assembled at specific locations. Approximately 1500 Work Numbers (production numbers) were allocated to the Fw 190D-9. Of these, almost 700 aircraft can be accounted for. However, of the later sub-types, Fw 190D-11/12/13/14/15 aircraft, with the Jumo 213E and F, and the Daimler-Benz 603E and LA engines, very few were completed prior to the war's end.

As a compliment to the aircraft's capabilities it should be noted that Fw 190Ds captured by the advancing Russian Army were painted with red stars and flown against the Luftwaffe. To many, the Fw 190D series is considered the best piston engine Luftwaffe fighter used in quantity during the Second World War.

Acknowledgments:

Diane Ryle	Bob Spaulding	Dave Goss	James V Crow
Vicki Laing	Steve Sheflin	Peter Petrick	Alan Ranger
Rich Dann	John Houston	Jerry Crandall	Donald Caldwell
Dave Wadman	Leroy Wahsum	Tom Tullis	Doug Champlin
John Bishop	Joyce Wahsum	Jeff Ethell	

USAF Museum, Wright-Patterson AFB, Ohio
Champlin Fighter Aces Museum, Mesa, AZ
Texas Air Museum, Rio Hondo, TX

ISBN 0-89747-374-4

If you have any photographs of aircraft, armor, soldiers or ships of any nation, particularly wartime snapshots, why not share them with us and help make Squadron/Signal's books all the more interesting and complete in the future. Any photograph sent to us will be copied and the original returned. The donor will be fully credited for any photos used. Please send them to:

Squadron/Signal Publications, Inc.
1115 Crowley Drive
Carrollton, TX 75011-5010

Если у вас есть фотографии самолётов, вооружения, солдат или кораблей любой страны, особенно, снимки времён войны, поделитесь с нами и помогите сделать новые книги издательства Эскадрон/Сигнал ещё интереснее. Мы переснимем ваши фотографии и вернём оригиналы. Имена приславших снимки будут сопровождать все опубликованные фотографии. Пожалуйста, присылайте фотографии по адресу:

Squadron/Signal Publications, Inc.
1115 Crowley Drive
Carrollton, TX 75011-5010

軍用機、装甲車両、兵士、軍艦などの写真を所持しておられる方はいらっしゃいませんか？どの国のものでも結構です。作戦中に撮影されたものが特に良いのです。Squadron/Signal社の出版する刊行物において、このような写真は内容を一層充実し、興味深くすることができます。当方にお送り頂いた写真は、複写の後お返しいたします。出版物中に写真を使用した場合は、必ず提供者のお名前を明記させて頂きます。お写真は下記にご送付ください。

Squadron/Signal Publications, Inc.
1115 Crowley Drive
Carrollton, TX 75011-5010

Front Cover: Lt Oscar Rom of IV/JG 3 and his wingman climb toward an American bomber stream as it heads deep into Germany.during the spring of 1945.

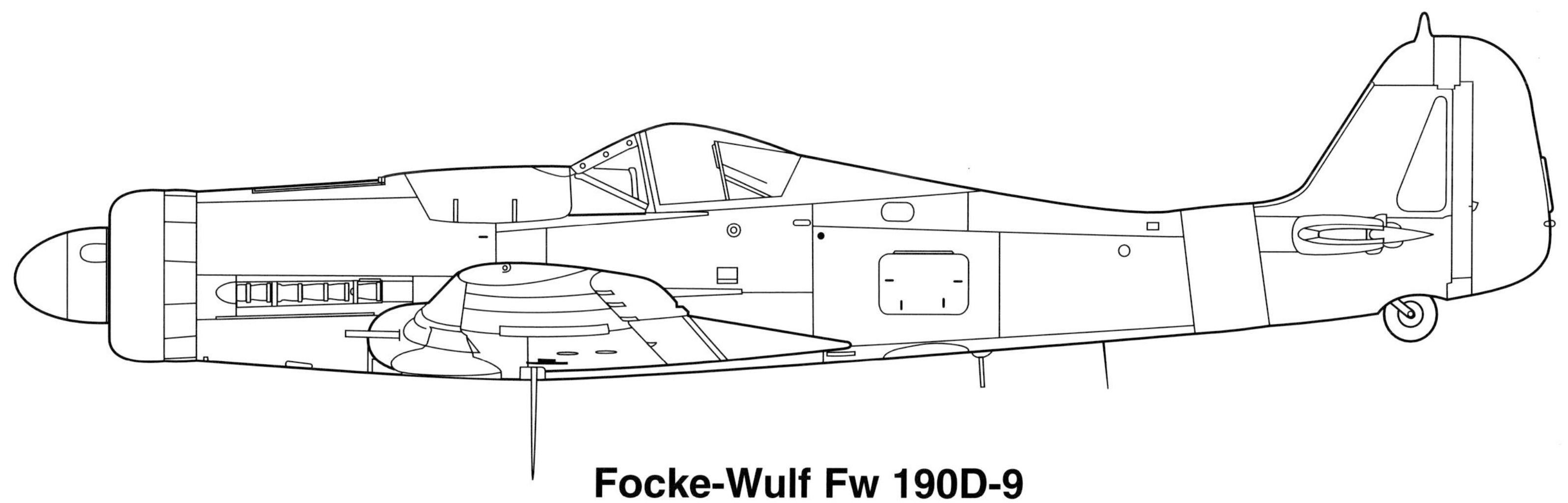

Ending up like most German aircraft during the spring and summer of 1945 — being stripped by souvenir hunters, White < 57 (W.Nr. 220011), an Fw 190D-11 is believed to have been originally assigned to the Stab General der Jagdflieger then assigned to the Würger Staffel of JV 44. Photographed during the summer of 1945 at Bad Worishofen, Germany. (Petrick via Wadman)

Focke-Wulf Fw 190D-9

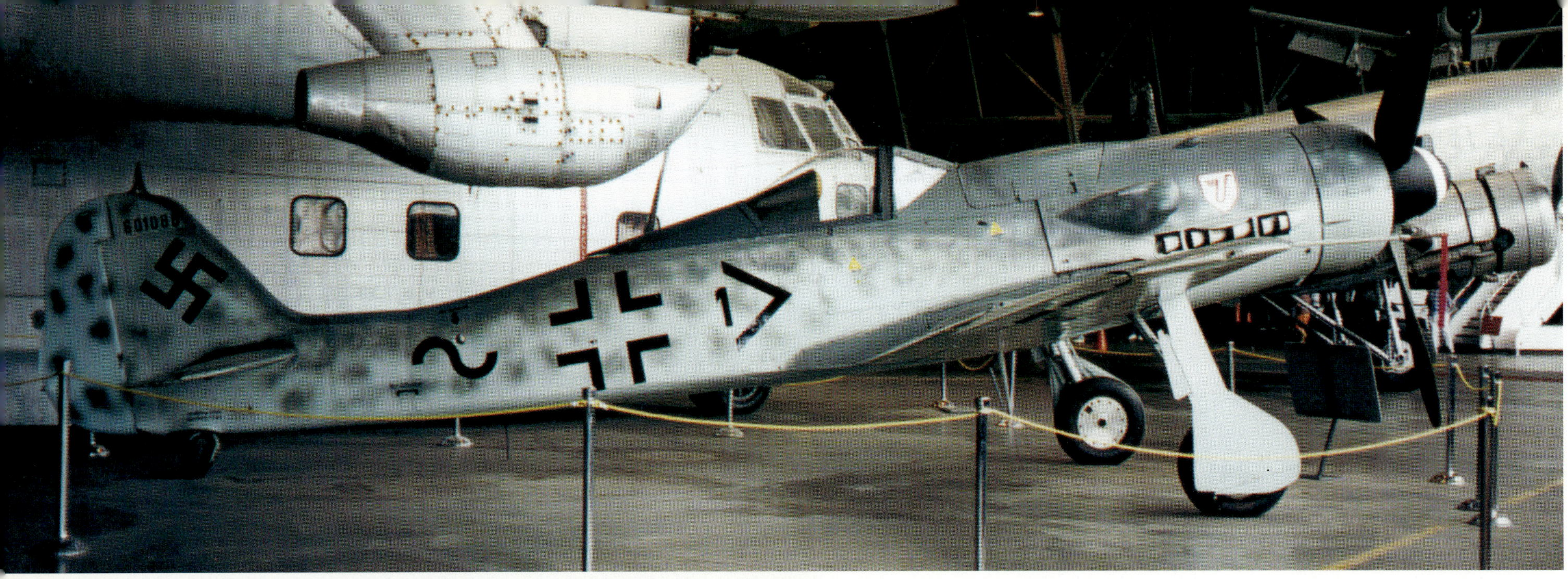

The Fw 190D-9 on display at the USAF Museum at Wright-Patterson AFB, Ohio. It is believed that this aircraft was used operationally by JG 26 and was surrendered to the RAF at Flensburg, then listed as either "USA-12" or "USA-15" when it made its way to the United States aboard HMS Reaper. This may be the Fw 190D-9 which flew six hours of test fights at Wright Field in 1946. The aircraft is now owned by the National Air and Space Museum and is on loan to the USAF Museum in Dayton. The paint scheme was for an aircraft flown by the technical officer of III\JG 3 'UDET'. (Author: Ryle)

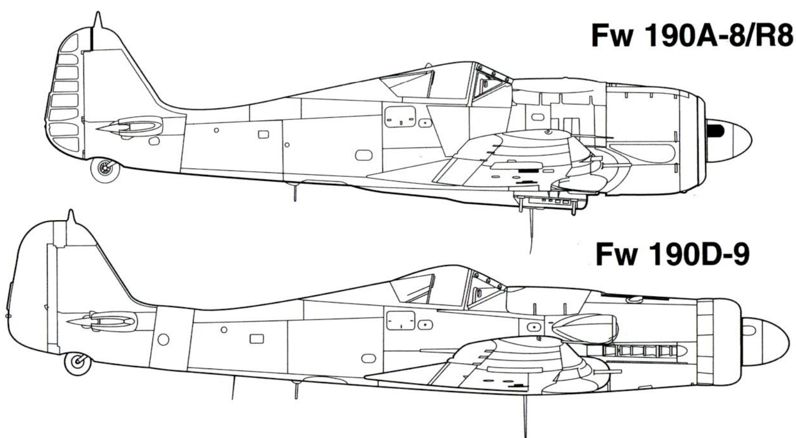

The smooth mating of the engine, fuselage and wing is evident at this angle as well as the dihedral of the wings. The propeller blades, however, are incorrect for this aircraft. (L & J Wahsum)

The Fw 190D-9 from the rear, the preferred view of Allied pilots. The taper from the thick forward fuselage to the thin tail assembly is evident. The tail wheel is turned 90 degrees to the right. (L & J Wahsum)

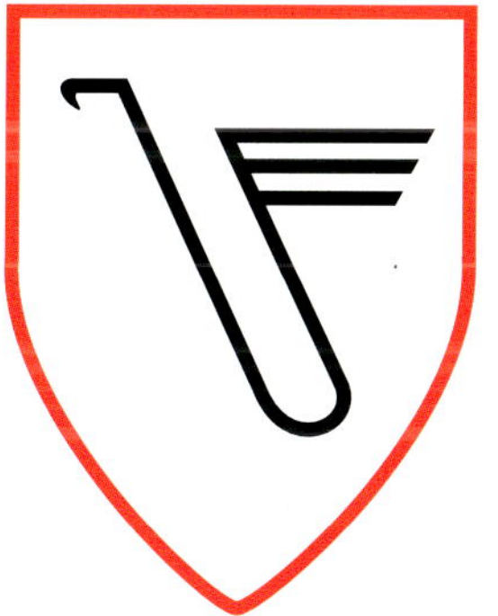

Jagdgeschwader 3 Udet

The starboard side of the fuselage showing the replica canopy (with the exterior hasp). The canopy's fit is not as close as it could be; further, the replica canopy has no rollers, so it will not slide. (L & J Wahsum)

(Above) The USAF Museum's FW 190D-9 under restoration. The wheels have been removed and the aircraft is on support stands with the lower engine panels removed and the side engine panels open. On the leading edge of the wing, at the landing gear connection point, the outboard 'cannon' panel has been removed. (USAF Museum via Tullis)

Fw 190D-9 Specifications

Powerplant:	Junkers Jumo 213A-1
	12 cylinder liquid cooled
	inline engine
Horse power	1,776 hp at take off
	1,600 hp at 18,000 ft
Armament	Two 20mm MG 151 cannons
	Two 13mm MG131 machine guns
Maximum Speed	426 mph at 21,650 ft
Wing span	34 ft 5 1/2 in
Length	33 ft 5 1/4 in

(Left) Like all restoration projects restoring the Fw 190D-9 was a labor of love. With the engine compartment side panels open the Jumo 213A engine and super charger were easily accessible for work to be done. The inside of the side panel contains extra bracing to support the bottom engine panel. (USAF Museum via Tullis)

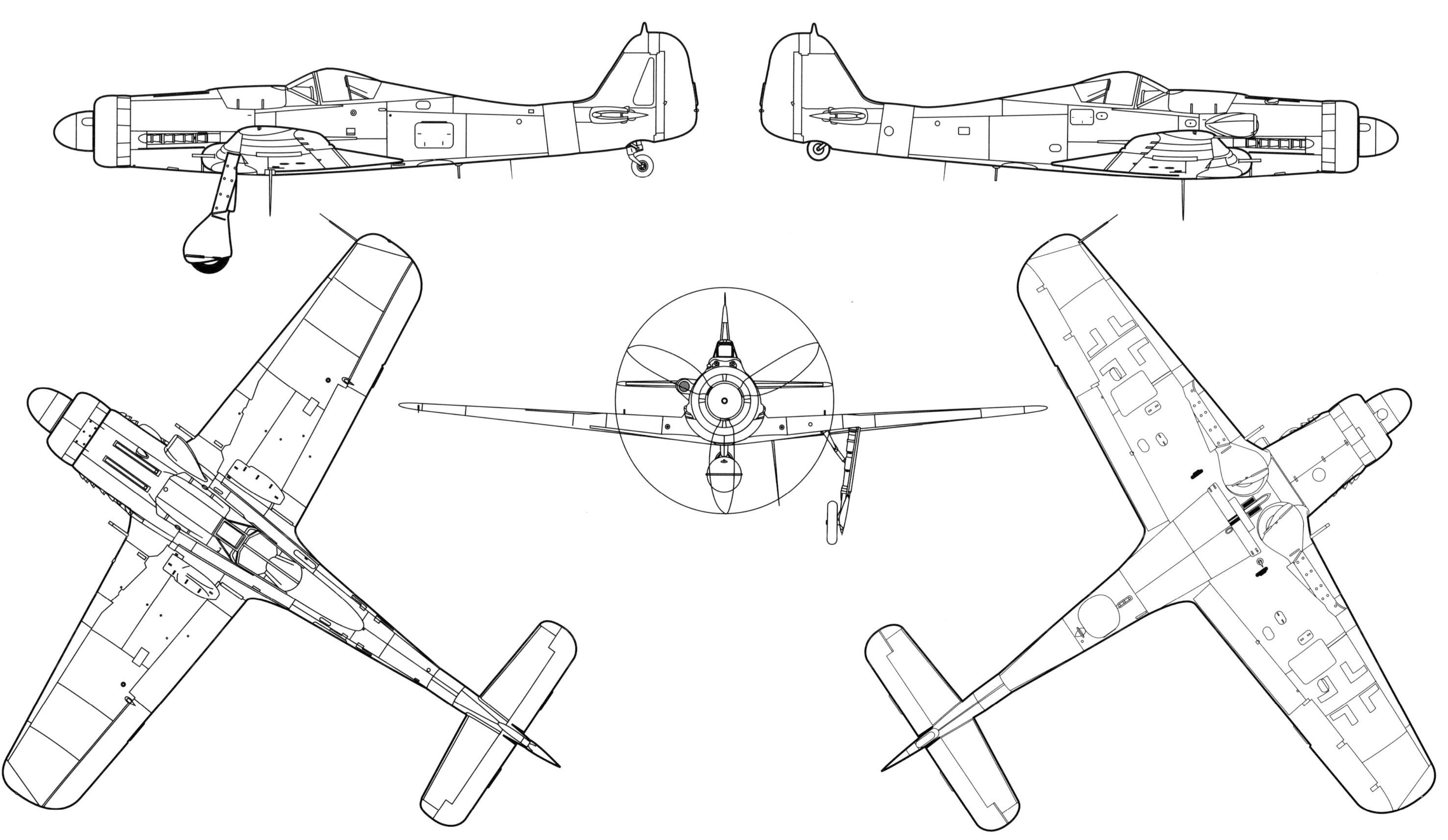

Focke-Wulf   Fw 190D-9

On the port side of fuselage is the aft fuselage access door. This door is original and has the correct four latches. (Author: Ryle)

Fuselage Access Door

Looking straight into the fuselage access opening, the auxiliary fuel tank (left) and the starter crank (right) readily stand out. On the opposite side of the fuselage the elevator control cables run along the side of the fuselage. (Author: Ryle)

(Above) Looking forward through the aft fuselage access door at the fuselage auxiliary 115 liter (25.3 gal) fuel tank located directly behind the cockpit. This tank did not have a cockpit indicator, and the pilot considered it empty when the rear tank of the two main fuel tanks, both located below the cockpit, indicated below 240 liters. (Author: Ryle)

(Above right) On the floor of the fuselage is the somewhat rounded door that also provided access to the auxiliary fuel tank. To save on strategic materials late in the war this was made of wood. The engine starter crank is clipped to the lower bulkhead just in front of the remote compass. (Author: Ryle)

(Right) Inside the fuselage looking aft at the remote compass. Along the interior are vertical stiffeners that provided strength to the fuselage skinning. (Author: Ryle)

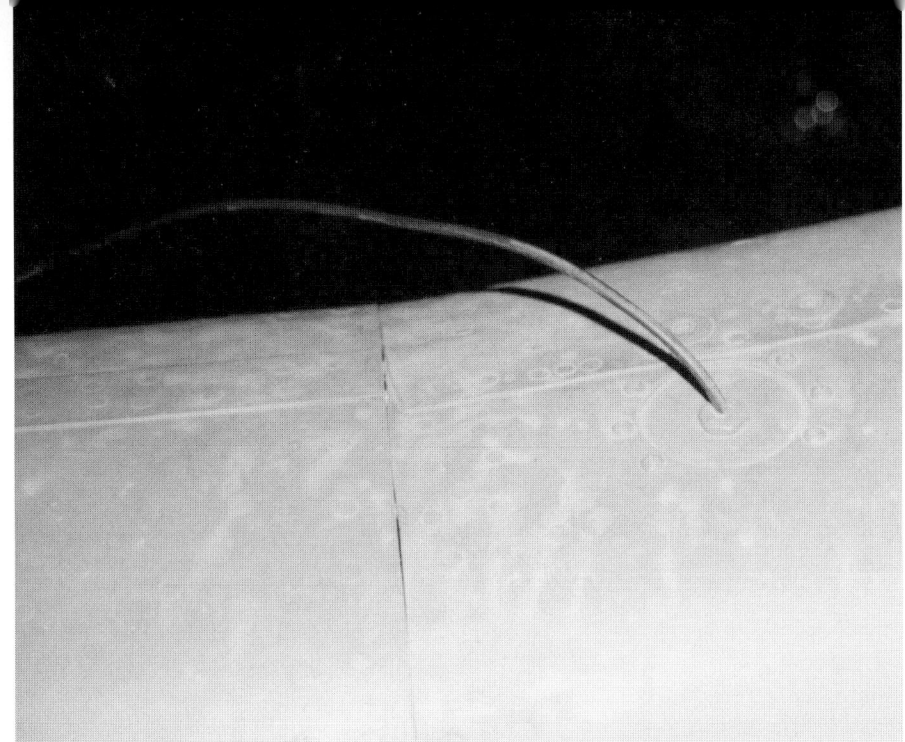

(Above) The vertical antenna wire's attachment point. There is no retraction unit to maintain tension on the antenna wire so it collapses unless the canopy is in the fully closed position. (Author: Ryle)

(Above left) This view of the spine of the aircraft somewhat distorts the fact that the fuselage extension plug, which extends the length of the D-9 series, does not change diameter as it approaches the tail assembly. The extension plug has a double upper seam and the fuselage spine seam is to the right of the centerline. (Author: Ryle)

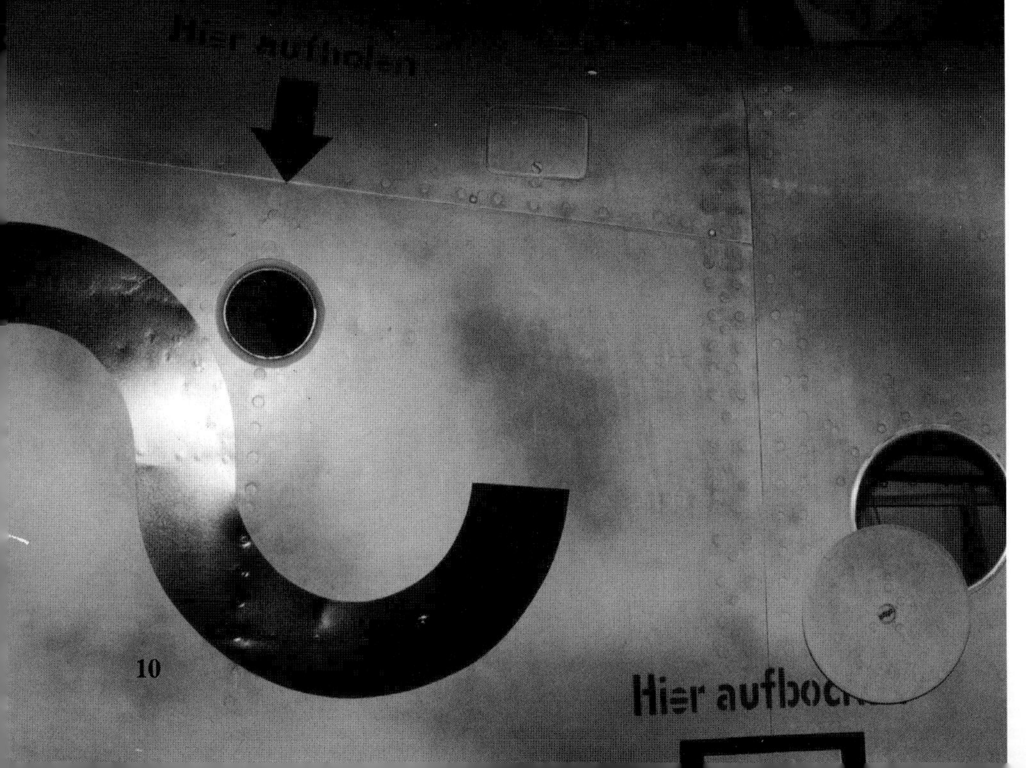

(Left) The port aft side of the fuselage showing the tie-down hole/lifting tube (which extends completely through the fuselage), with the arrow pointing toward it, and the opened access hole in the fuselage extension plug. (Author: Ryle)

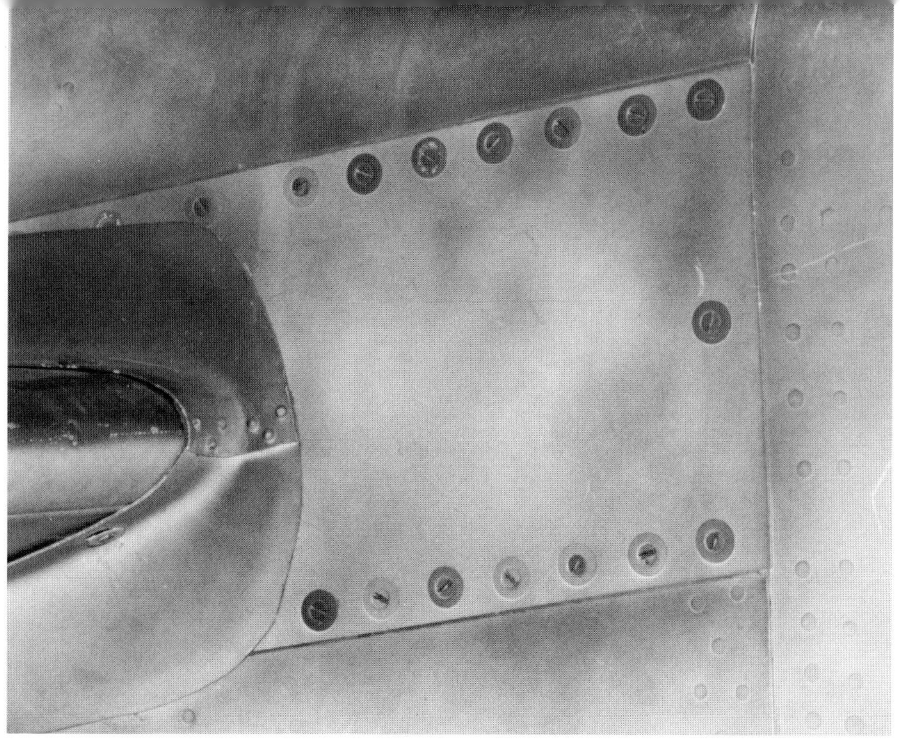

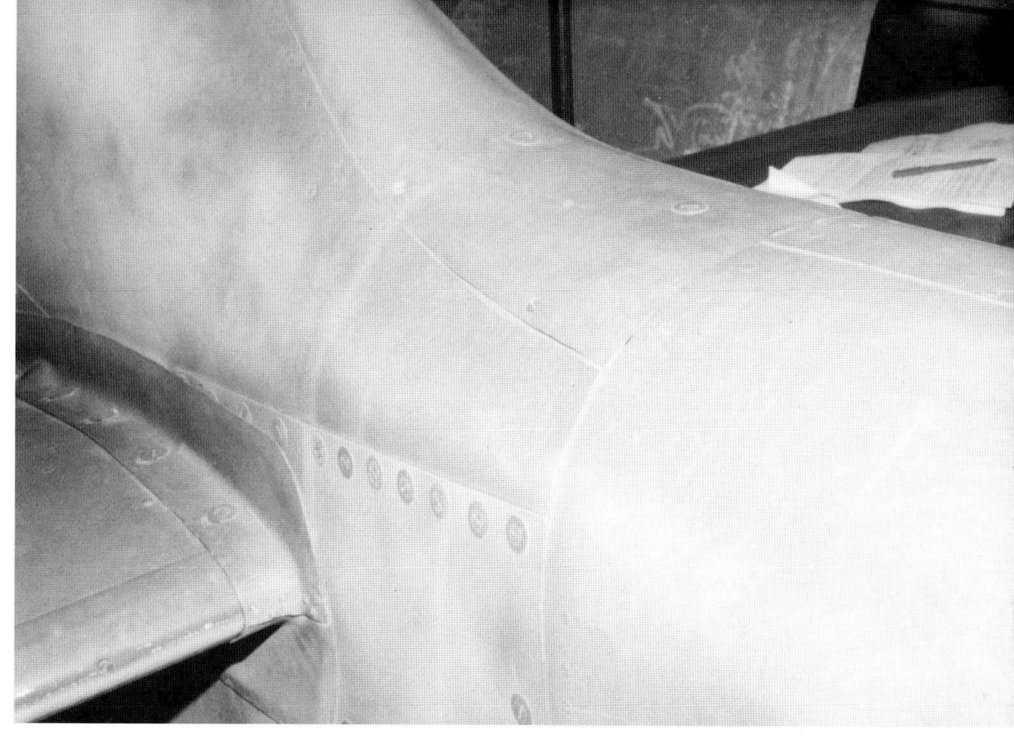

(Above) The panel immediately forward of the horizontal stabilizer is attached with screws and is removable. The faring on the stabilizer is not riveted because it moved with the stabilizer when trim adjustments were made. (J. Bishop)

(Above right) The leading edge of the vertical stabilizer was attached along its centerline with screws and was removable. (J. Bishop)

(Right) The plug used to extend the fuselage on all Fw 190D aircraft were not as well fitted as it is on this aircraft. And even as well fitted as it is here, it is not flush at all points. On the lower left of the fuselage aft of the plug a repair patch may be seen. (J. Bishop)

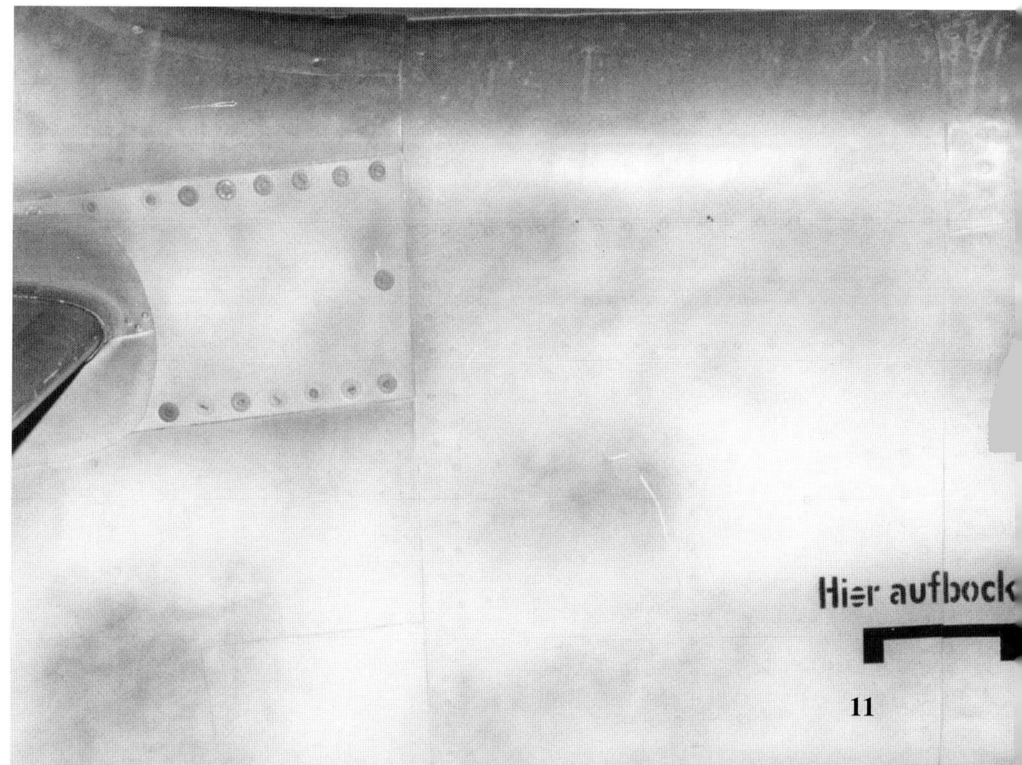

11

(Above) The fuel access hatch for the forward fuel tank is on the starboard side of the forward fuselage. An original fuel access hatch, it is hinged at the top. Just to the left of the yellow fuel triangle is the flare tube which extends from inside the cockpit. The rear of the supercharger intake can be seen on the right. (Author: Ryle)

(Above left) The radio access door on the starboard side of the aircraft just behind the rear fuel filler hatch. The three latches are in the closed position. (J. Bishop)

(Left) The three latches are opened and the radio access panel is raised to reveal the FuG 16Zy radio installed just behind the pilot's seat. (J. Bishop)

(Above)The lower starboard side of the fuselage looking aft. There are no external skin stiffeners on the tail prior to the tail wheel as are found on the later Fw 190D-13. (J. Bishop)

(Above right) The NASM machine on display at Dayton may have a replica rudder. Although the metal vertical fin and the cloth rudder are painted with the same paint (RLM 76 Light Blue Gray) the rudder appears to be a different tone, a somewhat common feature of Fw 190 aircraft. (L & J Wahsum)

(Right)The port side of tail assembly showing the horizontal stabilizer attachment. The small stiffener just above the rear edge of the stabilizer fairing is found on most late war Fw 190s (J. Bishop)

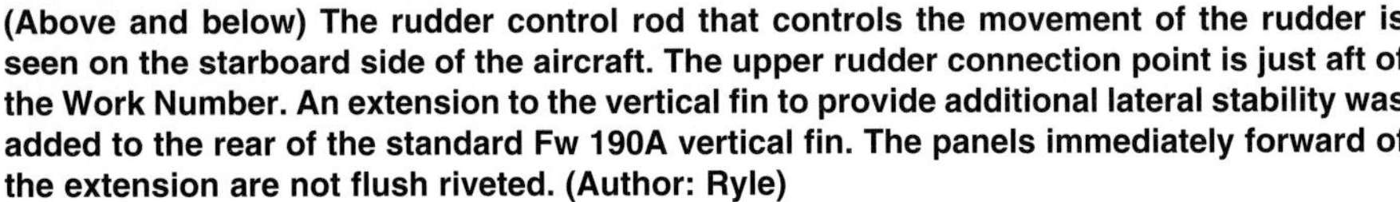

(Above and below) The rudder control rod that controls the movement of the rudder is seen on the starboard side of the aircraft. The upper rudder connection point is just aft of the Work Number. An extension to the vertical fin to provide additional lateral stability was added to the rear of the standard Fw 190A vertical fin. The panels immediately forward of the extension are not flush riveted. (Author: Ryle)

The canopy is open so the antenna wire drapes down slack. The aircraft's work number (601088) indicates it was built in a production batch of eighty aircraft that were some of the last Fw 190s to be produced before the end of the war. (Author: Ryle)

With the canopy in the closed position the antenna wire is pulled taught. The small spring is to maintain tension. (Author: Ryle)

The tail wheel fork is a late war welded type with prominent rough weld lines. As the war got more desperate such things as deburring weld joints were ignored especially when they did not affect the functioning of the equipment. With no original available an American tail wheel and tire have been substituted. An unusual feature is the addition of a fairing around the tail wheel opening. (Author: Ryle)

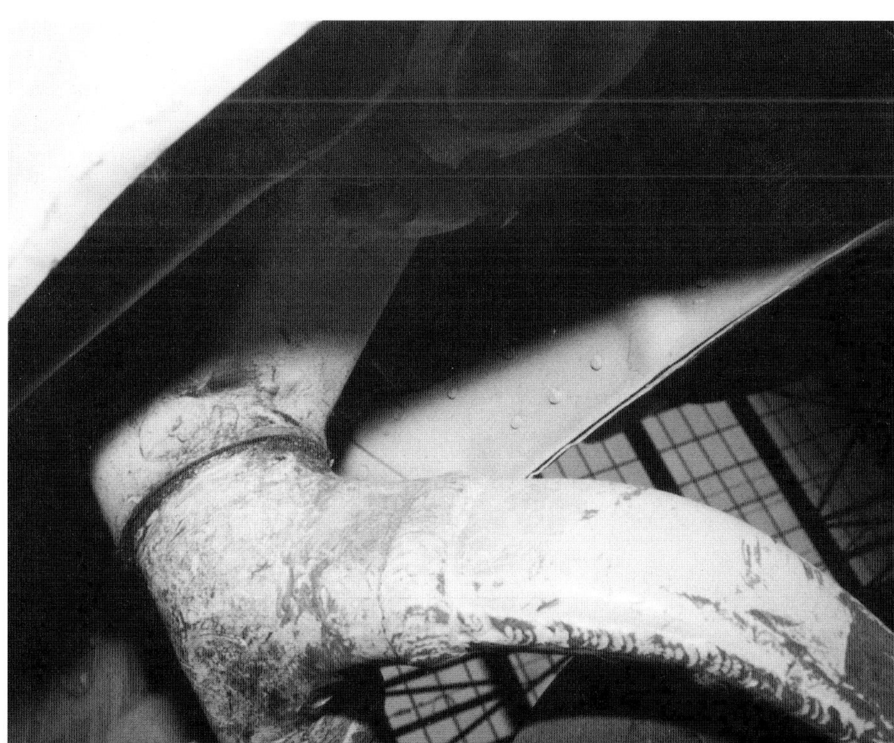

The replica canopy fits poorly to the armored windscreen. The small tube on the front of the windscreen is the windscreen (cleaning) spray tube which cleaned the windscreen with fuel from the fuel line running to the fuel pressure gauge in the cockpit. It has broken and slipped down, but its lower attachment can clearly be seen. (L & J Wahsum)

Embedded in the heavy glass of the armored windscreen are the small red strips of the electric anti-ice system essential to high altitude operations. The fittings (bolts) along the top edge of the windscreen are double, single, double. Other windscreen bolts have been documented as double, double and double. (Author: Ryle)

15

(Above) Forward of the throttle lever is the trim indicator, starter button, and the instrument light dimmer. On the lower instrument panel is the IFF panel, above that is the landing gear manual extension and the red knobbed handle is the manual fuel tank selector lever. (Author: Ryle)

(Left) The left console, like the right, is dusty, but original. The white knobbed plunger at the rear of the console is the primer fuel pump handle. The Brown plug-in forward of the primer is for the pilot's headset. The two turn knobs are controls for the FuG 16ZY radio. Further forward are the landing gear and flap actuator buttons with the horizontal stabilizer trim switch to their right. The large white knob is on the throttle lever. (Author: Ryle)

(Below) The throttle friction knob extends from the bottom of the left console. The control stick has a boot installed around its bottom just above the elevator control rod coming out of the boot to the right console. (Author: Ryle)

(Above) The upper and lower instrument panels are surrounded by a leather cushioned combing. On the upper left, just under the combing, are the ammunition counters (which are missing) and to the right of the counters is the Revi 16 gun sight (not installed) mount. To the right of the mount is the AFN 2 homing indicator used for instrument approaches. (Author: Ryle)

(Right) The right side panel circuit breaker switches, the starter switch, canopy actuator drive wheel (on side wall of cockpit). The map case, with its leather strap can be seen on the lower side wall of the right console. (Author: Ryle)

(Below) The forward right section of the Fw 190D-9 cockpit. The differences in the upper and the lower recessed instrument panel are well defined. On the right side of the lower instrument panel is the flare tube and the oxygen instrument group. The missing instrument on the lower panel just below and to the right of the flare chute is a clock (Author: Ryle)

The seat was positioned at the very rear of the cockpit against the rear wall. The shelf built into the back supported the pilot's parachute. The white button to the right of the seat is the oxygen regulator. The canopy slide track can be seen above the seat. (Author: Ryle)

(Above and below) The decking at the rear of the cockpit, under which sits the radio equipment. The piece running across the rear of the cockpit immediately behind the seat is the 'shoulder armor' and is 5mm thick. The access door behind the shoulder armor can be opened and used as the pilot's storage compartment. This is one of several different styles of this door. (Author: Ryle)

The shoulder strap attachment bars are bolted and riveted to the lower face of the shoulder armor plate just above the seat back. Both of these attachment bars face to the left; it is not known if this procedure was intentional, accidental, or due to wartime conditions. (Author: Ryle)

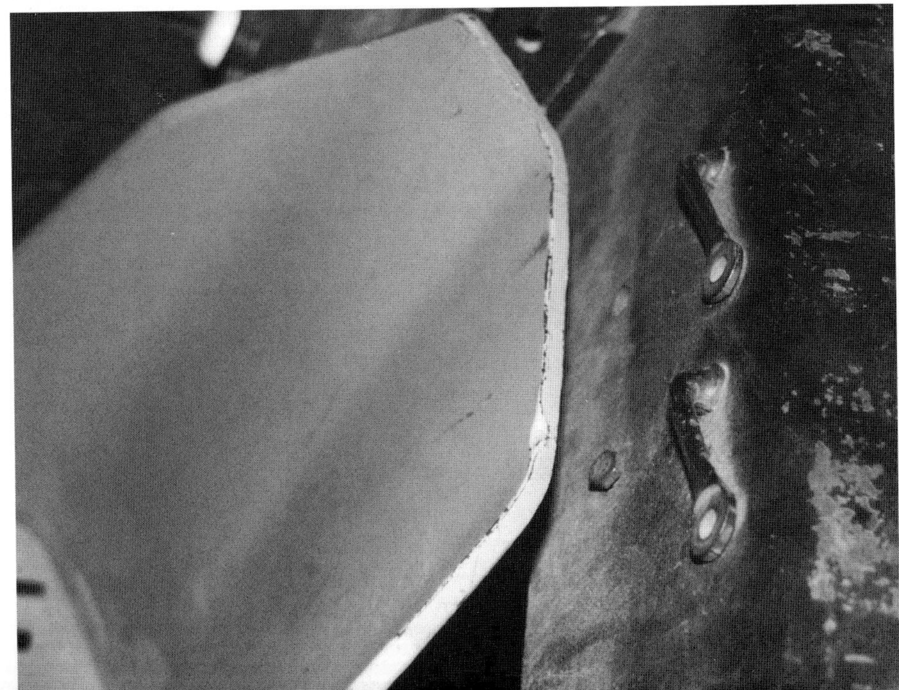

18

The upper engine panel has machine gun troughs welded in place. The hole at front of the bulged machine gun cover is for the engine starter crank. (J. Bishop)

The bulged machine gun cover has two latches on each side. This cover was in three sections with the center section overlapping the outside sections and riveted together. (J. Bishop)

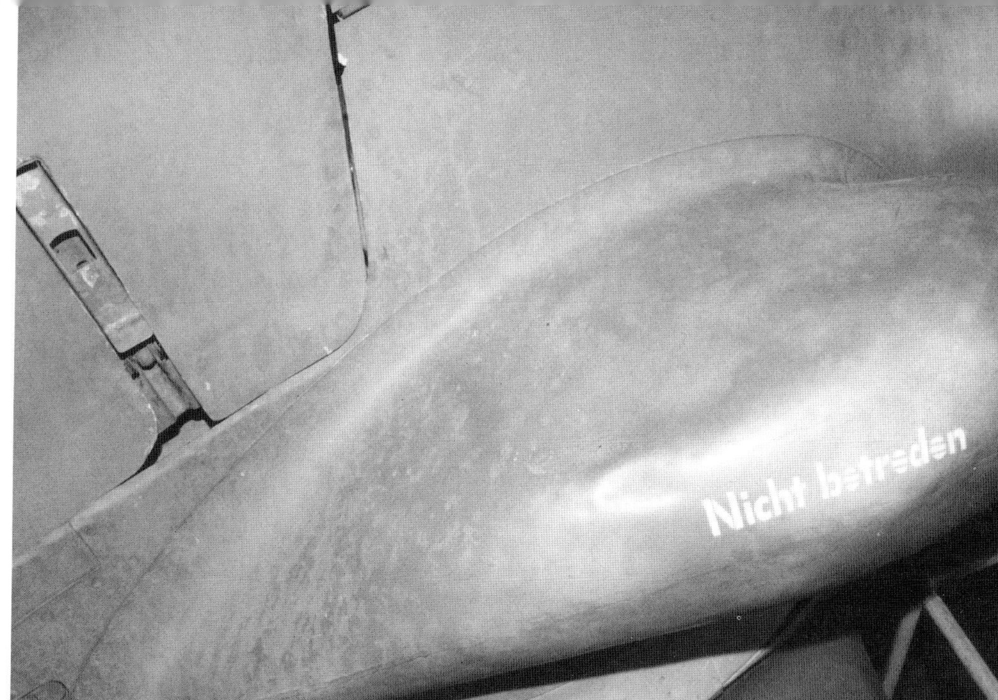

The weld line divides the supercharger intake into upper and lower halves. The words *Nicht betreten* translates as "No Step". (Author: Ryle)

The Fw 190D series had the engine supercharger air intake on the starboard side of the fuselage. The intake's opening is perfectly round. The intake is made from several pieces of aluminum welded together and the completed assembly is flush riveted to the engine panel. (Author: Ryle)

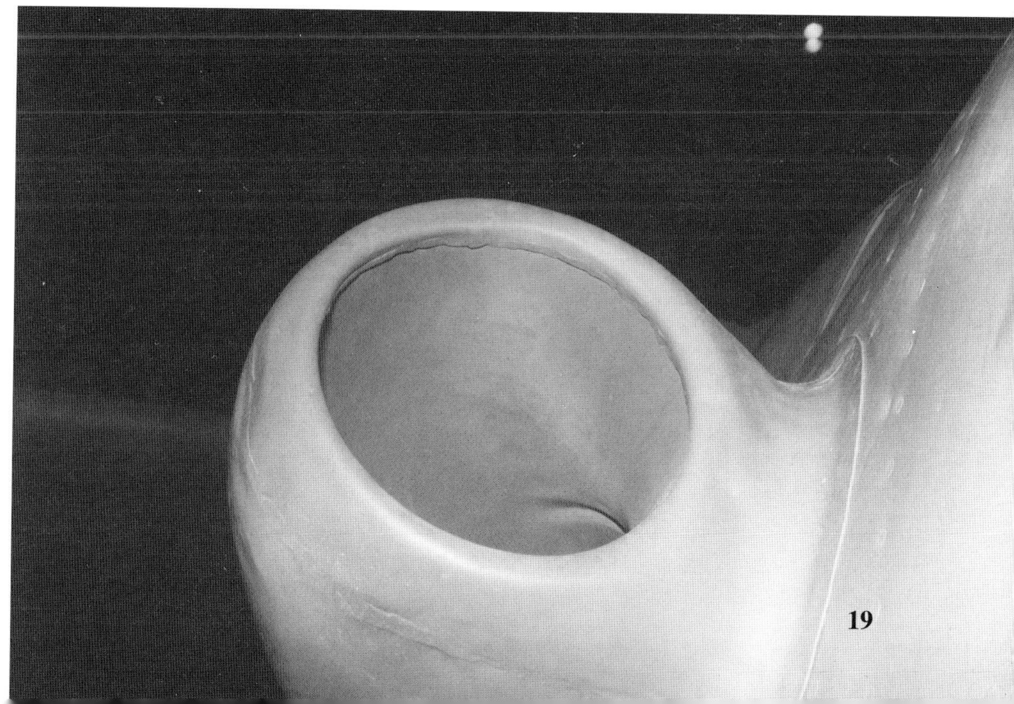

(Above) The oval shaped exhausts pipes have weld lines on both the front and back side of each exhaust. The rod extending upward from the wing top is the visual wheel position indicator rod. The top of the rod is usually painted red over a bottom of white. (J. Bishop)

(Above left) The forward starboard side of the Fw 190D-9 displayed at the USAF Museum carries the flying U emblem of JG 3 "Udet". The smooth fit of the in-line engine installed in a radial engine designed airframe is evident. The Jumo 213A engine delivered 1,770 Ps(hp)2 at takeoff. The Fw 190D-9 was capable of 426mph at 21,654ft and had a normal range of 503 miles. (Author: Ryle)

(Left) The poor late war fit of the bulged cowl gun cover panel is obvious and was common to late war Fw 190 aircraft. An external stiffener for D series aircraft has been added to the fuselage just below the cowling gun cover and above the wing root 20mm cannon cover. (J. Bishop)

Fresh air for the cockpit was provided by an intake scoop located on the upper starboard rear engine panel in front of and just below the 13mm machine gun port. (J. Bishop)

(Above right) The starboard side of the lower engine cowling just behind the cowl flaps is the coolant overflow pipe. The opening around the exhausts is somewhat larger at the front than at its rear. (J.Bishop)

The spinner is a reproduction and the propeller blades are not the VS-111 or VS-9 blades specified for the Fw 190D-9. The circular radiator of the Fw 190D-9 can be seen behind the reproduction spinner. (J. Bishop)

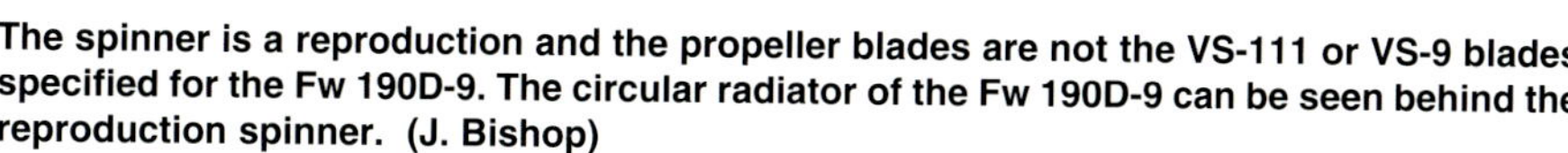

The lower engine cowling is in two panels, the starboard side and the port side with both the coolant and oil overflow lines exiting through the starboard panel. The cowling radiator flaps are fully closed and fit tightly. (J. Bishop)

(Right) A small patch has been applied to the bottom of the radiator cowling just in front of the bottom most cowl flap. The bottom radiator seam line and the seam line of the engine panels are almost, but not quite, in-line. (J. Bishop)

The first of the three latches is missing on the lower engine panels. To help provide a tight seal the lower panels have an internal strip filling the seam. The round panel on the port panel is an access door. (J. Bishop)

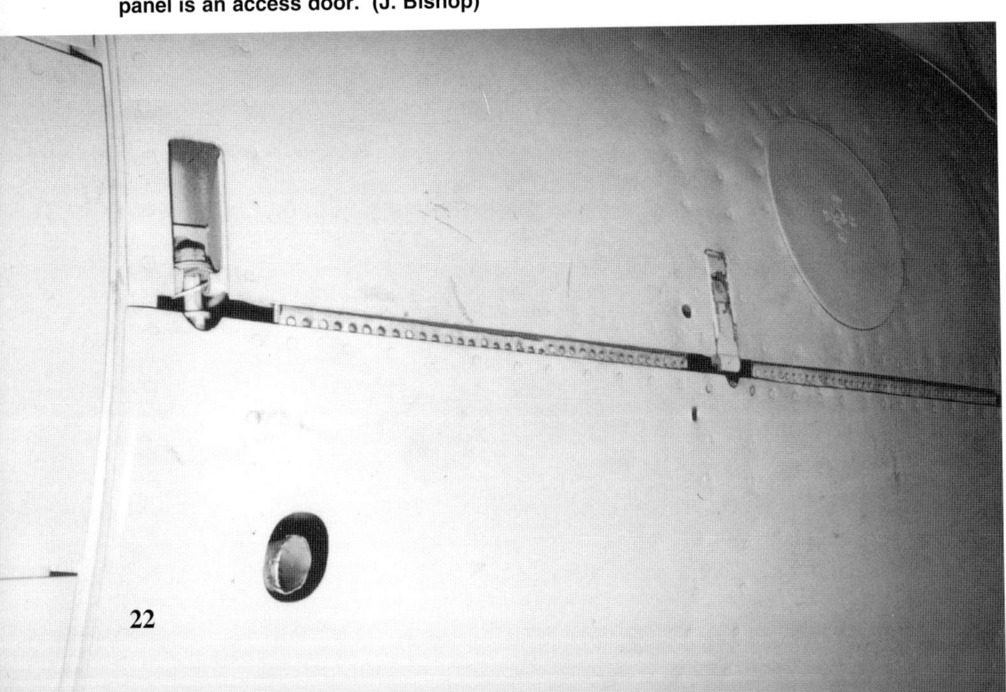

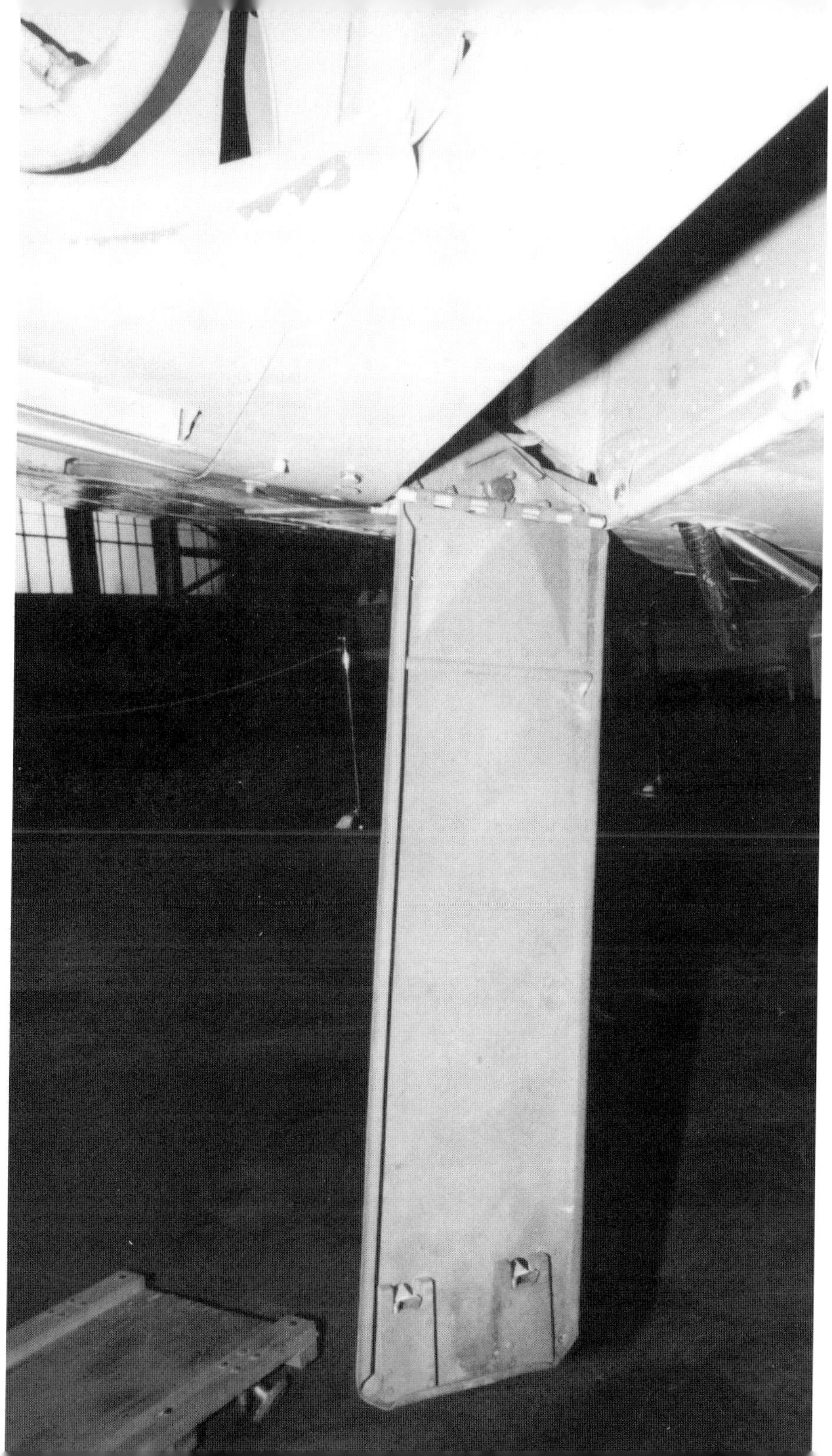

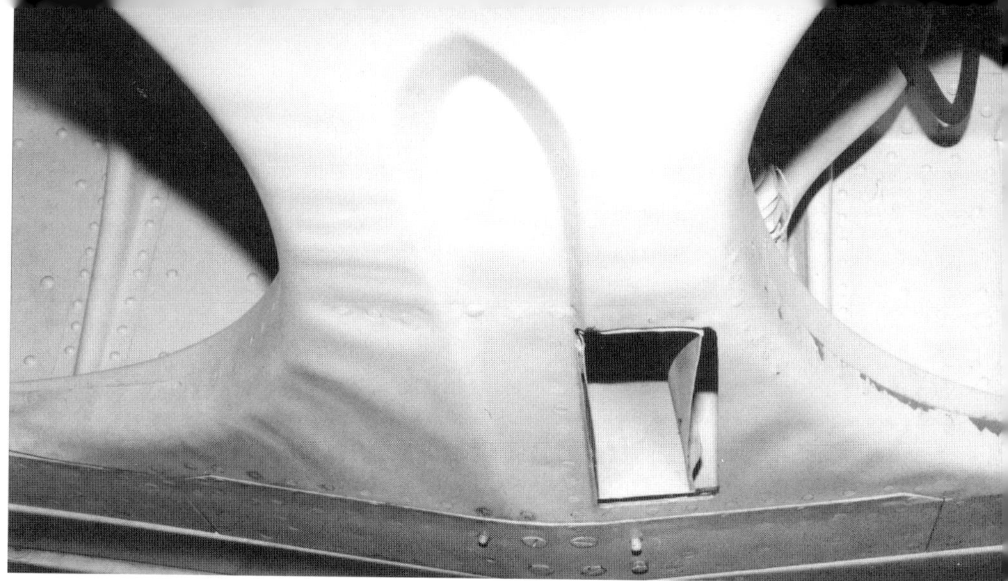

(Above) The ejection port for an engine mounted cannon is just to the port side of centerline. The indentation on the centerline is an aerodynamic feature designed to accommodate the forward portion of the or ETC 504 drop tank/bomb rack. This center panel is a single stamped part and the wrinkles from the stamping can be seen. (Author: Ryle)

(Left and below) On the wing bottom, just aft of the wheel well is one of the two access panels for the wing root 20mm cannon ammo trays. Two 250 round ammo trays were loaded and unloaded through theses panels which hinged at the center. The fuel tank vents are located directly behind these doors. (J. Bishop)

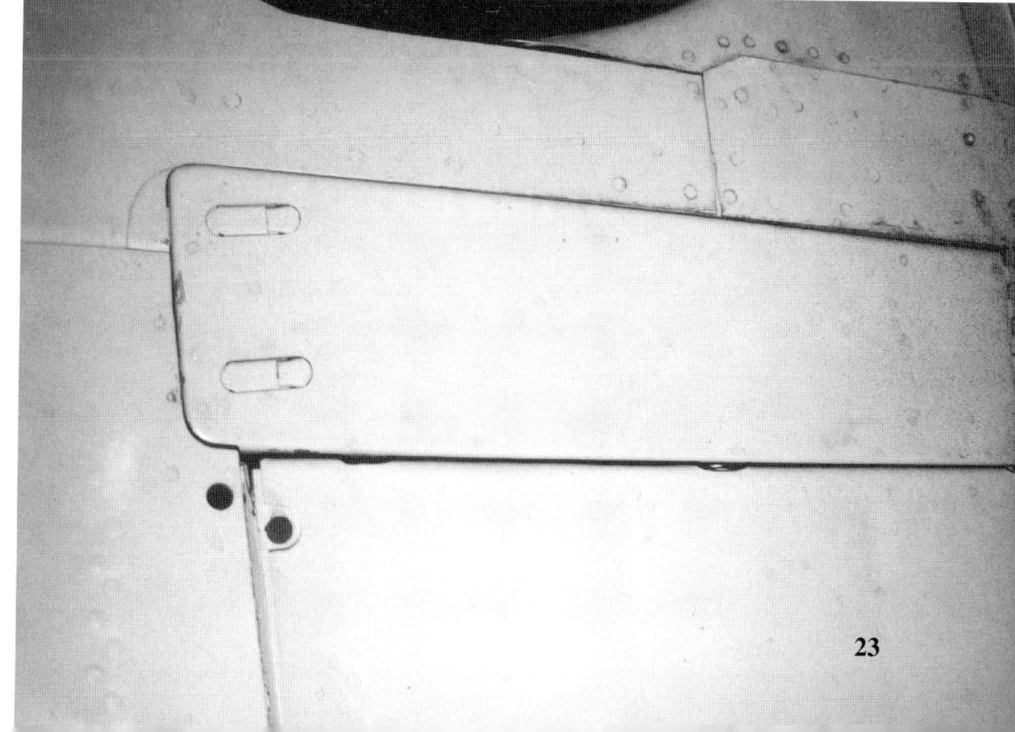

(Above) The port wing root fillet and the 20mm cannon access panel are both bolted to the fuselage with the cannon panel having a hinge just below the bolts. The wear marks on the wing are from museum personnel climbing on and off the aircraft — operational aircraft would have the same wear marks. (Author: Ryle)

(Below and Right) The port wing root cannon access panel in the open position. The 20mm cannon is not installed affording a look at the various items under and around the MG 151. The wiring bundle coming out of the fuselage is part of the electrical system for cocking and firing the cannons. The gap at the front of the gun bay is for the 20mm ammunition and its feed chute. (Author: Ryle)

Just below the upper cowl gun panel the port cowling engine panel latches are in the open position. The hinged wing gun bay door is fully open. (J. Bishop)

(Above and below) The port wing leading edge showing the empty wing root cannon port and the gun camera port. While the 20mm cannon port was produced as a part of the wing's leading edge panel, the camera port is a separate piece rivited into the leading edge of the wing panel. The glass cover on the camera port (missing) was exchangeable for a colored light filter. (D. Ryle)

The access panel was bulged to accommodate the MG 151 20mm cannon. The access panel is attached to the fuselage with nine small screws, the "piano" hinge may be seen just below the screws. (J. Bishop)

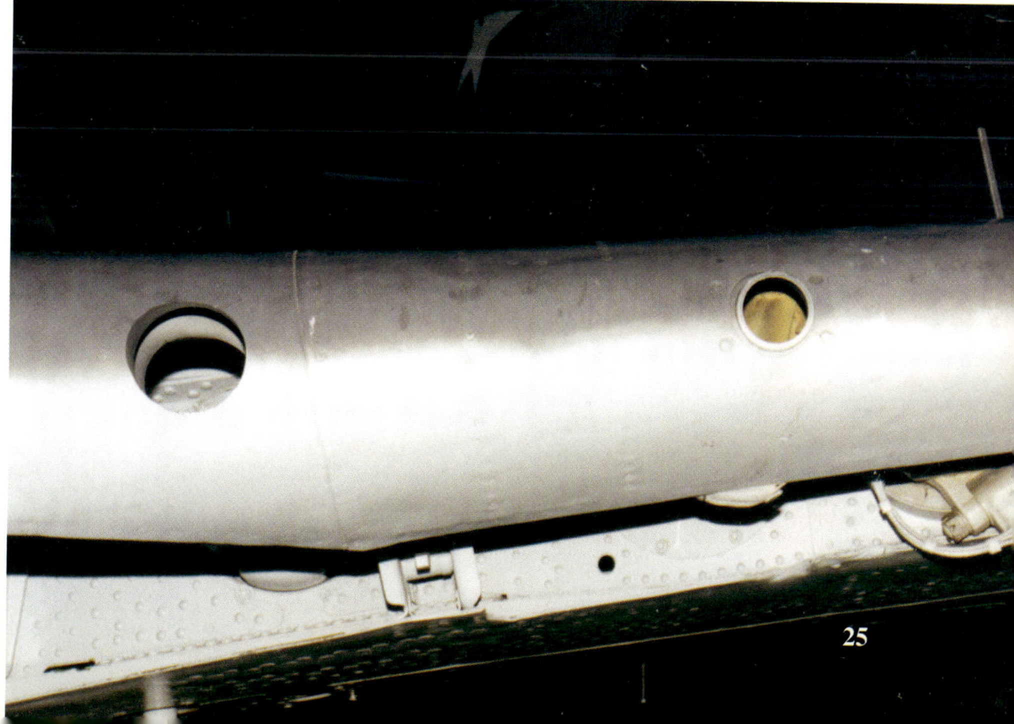

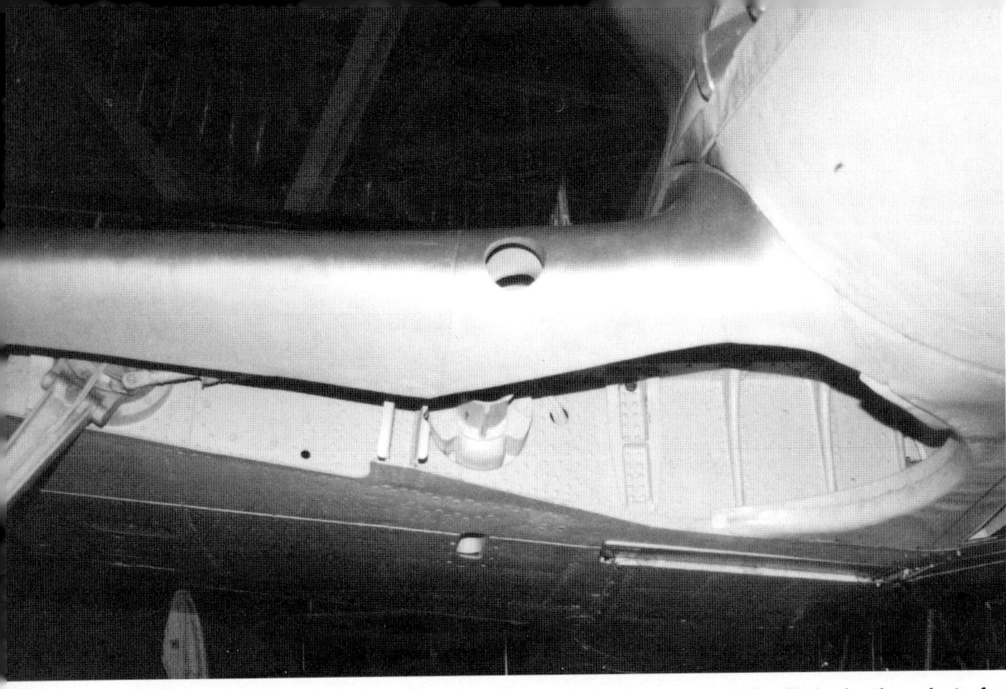

(Above and Below) The starboard wheel well. The spent cartridge/link ejection chute for the wing root cannon is on the bottom of the wing directly behind the gun port. An unusual feature of this ejection port is that it is "race track" in shape and does not have the smaller, outboard, ejection section for link disposal. (Author: Ryle)

(Above and below) The starboard wing leading edge with its wing root 20mm gun port. The Mg 151 cannons (not installed here) were mounted so close to the fuselage that they had to be twin synchronized (VIA DSG 3 AL and 2 ZS 2a ignition coils) to fire through the propeller arc. (Author: Ryle)

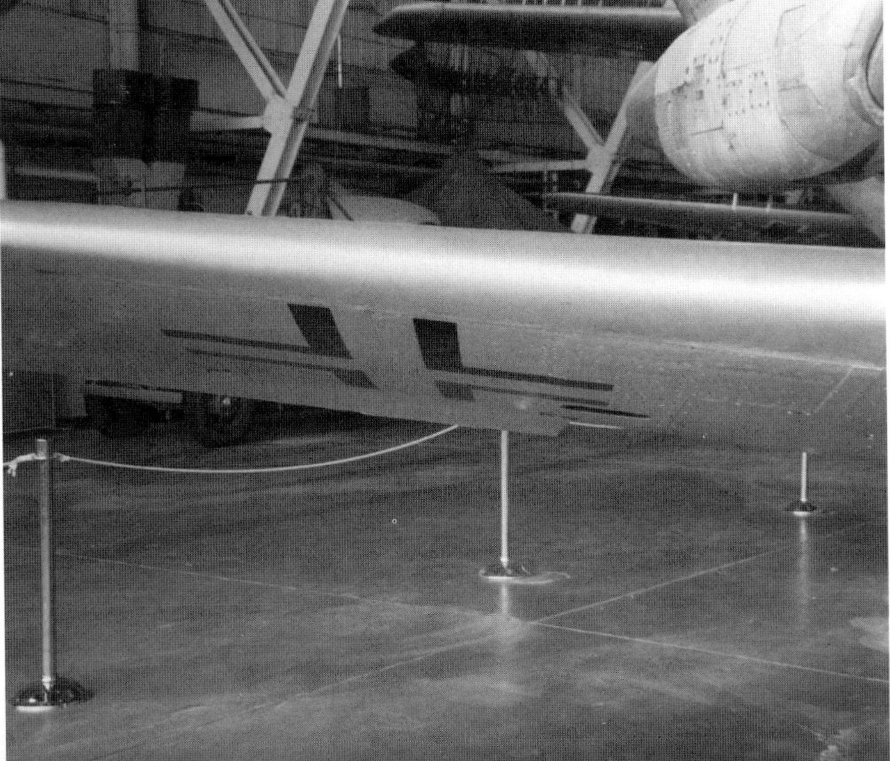

(Above) The wing had a three piece leading edge. This wing apears to have been manufactured specifically for late-war Fw 190s. The leading edge panels just outside the main gear do not have cannon ports or covered over cannon ports. (Author: Ryle)

(Right) The upper surface of the starboard wing showing the uncovered aileron control fittings, the landing gear position indicator and the overall wing construction. (Author: Ryle)

(Below) The aileron control rod fitting on the inner most portion of the aileron. This is a welded type. Most were cast. (Author: Ryle)

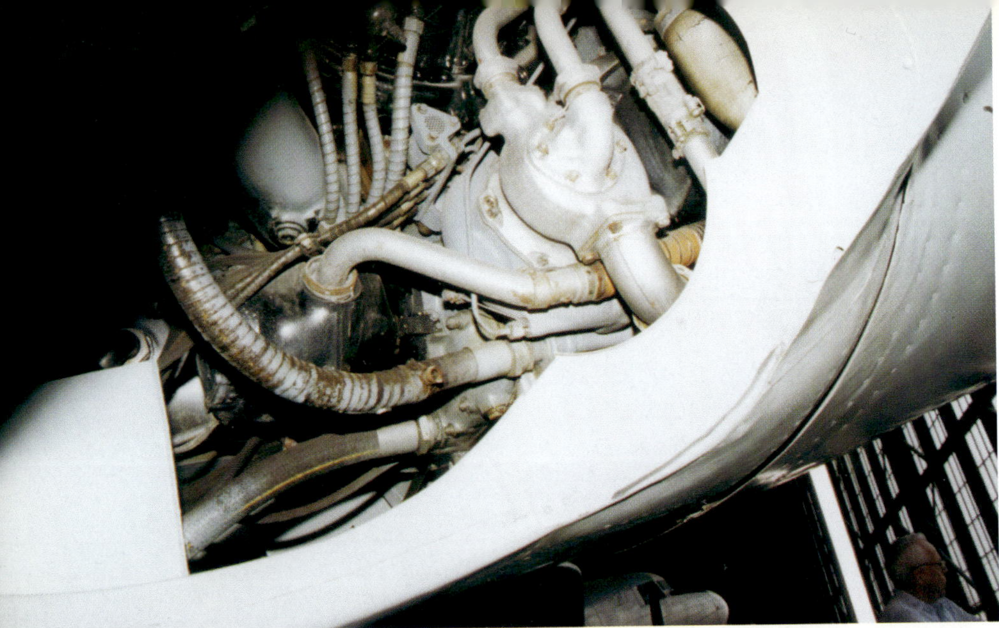

The starboard main wheel well contains a great deal of the lower engine plumbing. (J. Bishop)

Looking into the starboard wheel well the aluminum fuel filter is mounted in an inset on the right side of the firewall. To the right are the brackets for the 400 round ammo boxes for the cowling Mg 131 13mm machine guns and to the left is the motor mount and its attachment to the firewall. (Author: Ryle)

At the top of the port wheel well's open center can be seen the lower edge of the engine's unpainted oil tank and engine plumbing. Painted a Blue Gray color part of the throttle control linkage can be seen just behind the oil tank. (J. Bishop)

The port wheel well looking to the rear at the main wing spar, the throttle control linkages are at the top and the brass/link ejection port runs through the center of the wheel well exiting between the wheel wells. This configuration was designed for a center (engine) mounted cannon, which was not installed on the Fw 190D-9. (J. Bishop)

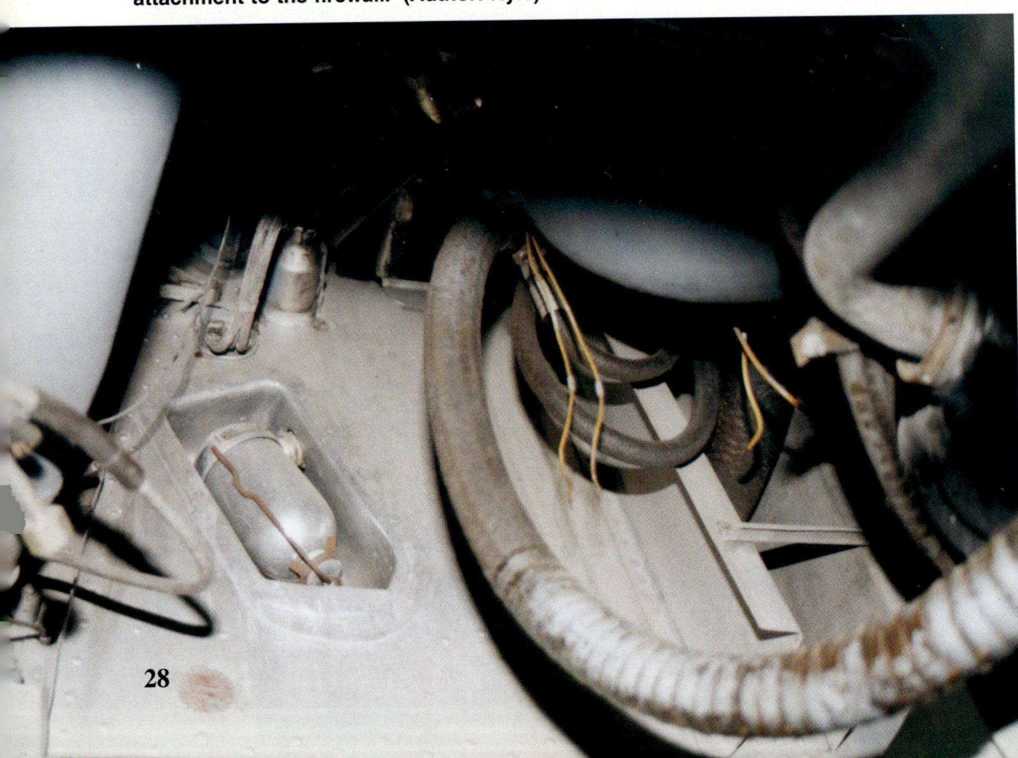

(Above) The construction of the starboard wheel well's forward wall with its electrical and brake lines are seen to advantage. (Author: Ryle)

(Right and below)The 20mm wing root gun mount coming out of the main spar. The pattern on the upper portion of the well are stiffeners stamped into the panel. A landing gear up-lock should be between the two braces outboard of the gun mount, but it is missing. (Author: Ryle)

(Above) The port wing flap in the up position. The flaps of the Fw 190 were electrically actuated by a drive motor push rod connected to the flaps central attachment fitting. The flaps were set at 13 (+or- 2) degrees for takeoff and 58 (+or- 3) degrees for landing. (Author: Ryle)

(Left) The morane antenna of the FuG 16ZY radio equipment was installed in the bottom of the wing just behind the port landing gear between the wing root 20mm ejection port and the wing root 20mm ammo tray loading panel. (Author: Ryle)

(Below) Panels were installed to cover the outboard wing cannon bays since the outboard cannon were not fitted to the Fw 190D-9, nor to the Fw 190D-13. The panel functioned only as a cover. (Author: Ryle)

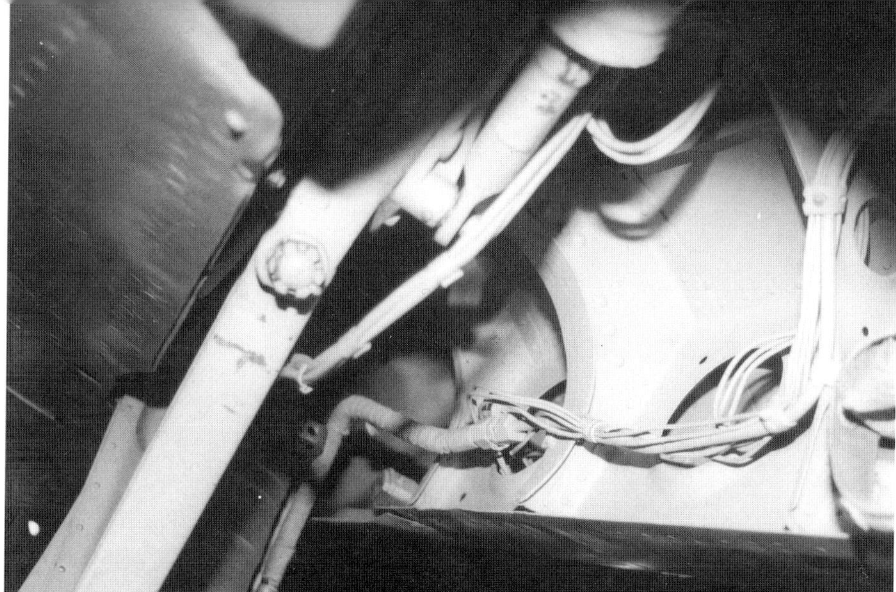

(Above and right) The forward wall of the port wheel well looking at the gun camera mount. When the pilot pressed the firing button for the wing root cannon the camera would start rolling. The gun camera, a BSK 16 16mm movie camera, was rarely installed. When the gun camera was installed, it was protected by a canvas cover. The over-sprayed remains of this cover are still installed. (Author: Ryle)

The port wheel well with the 20mm cannon mount in the back wall and the gear up-lock assembly to its right. The color of the wheel well is an RLM 76 Gray. A late war wheel well might be painted one of the following colors: RLM 02, 66, 76, 77 (primer Gray) or left unpainted in natural metal. (Author: Ryle)

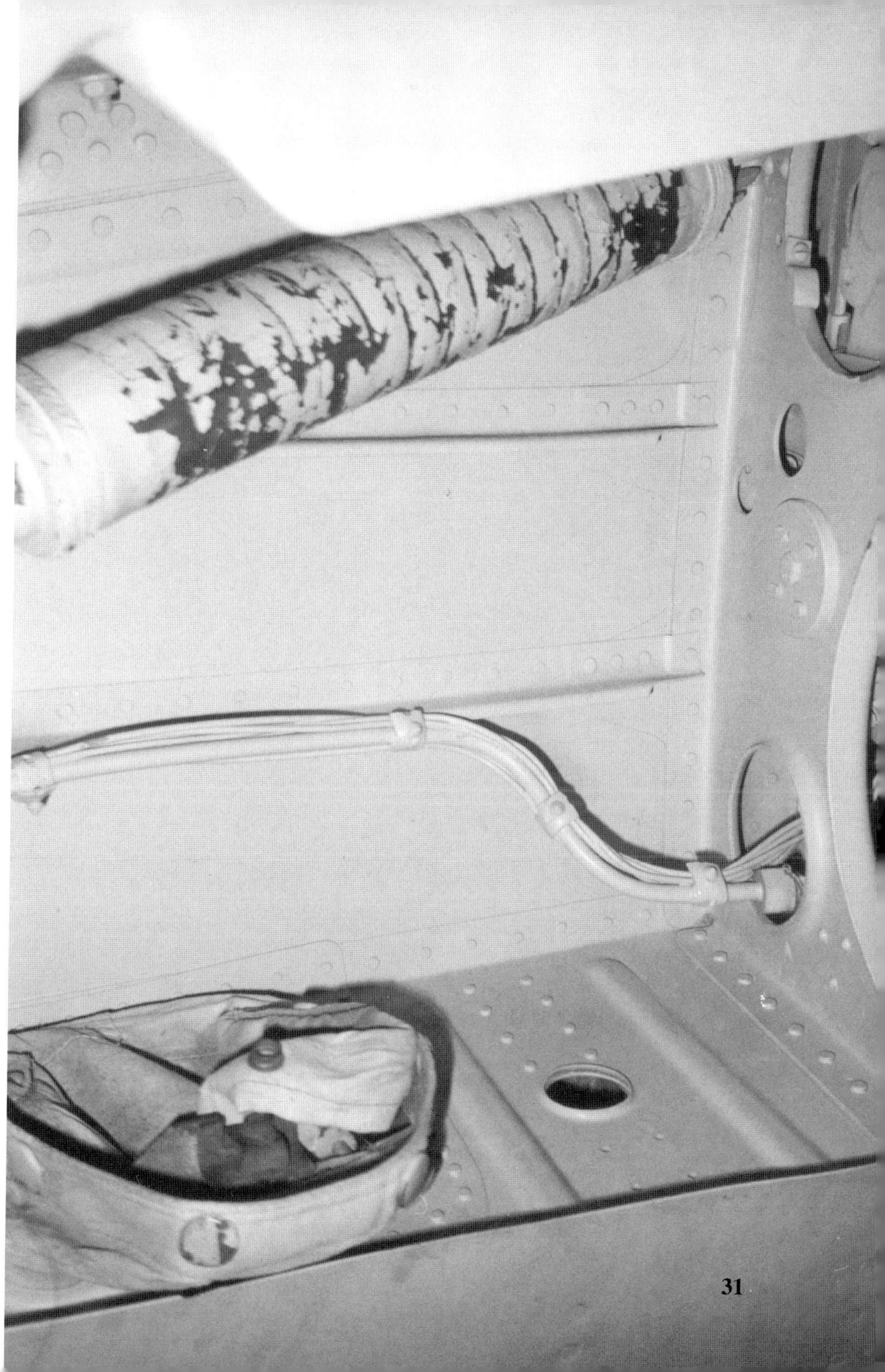

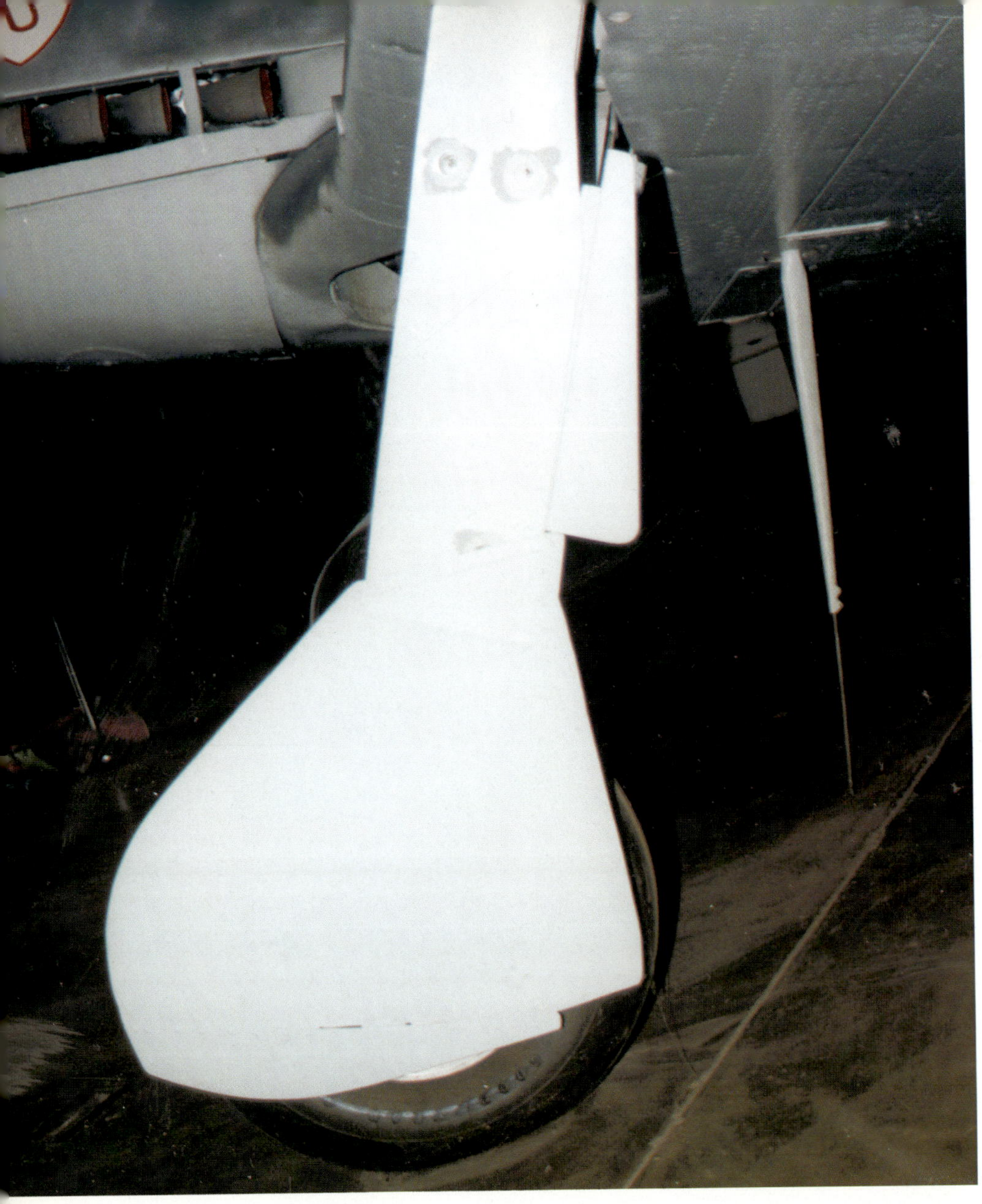

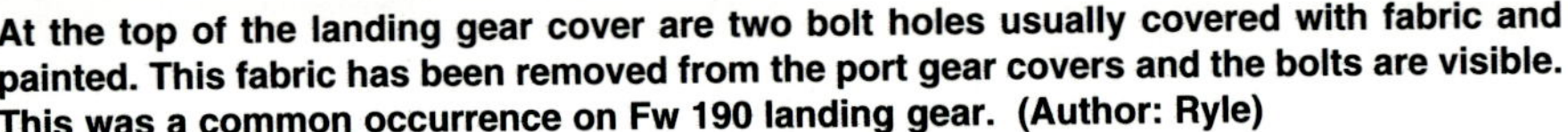

At the top of the landing gear cover are two bolt holes usually covered with fabric and painted. This fabric has been removed from the port gear covers and the bolts are visible. This was a common occurrence on Fw 190 landing gear. (Author: Ryle)

(Right) The forward side of the starboard landing gear. The metal line running down the strut is the brake line, which has been disconnected from the wheel and turned up at the bottom. (Author: Ryle)

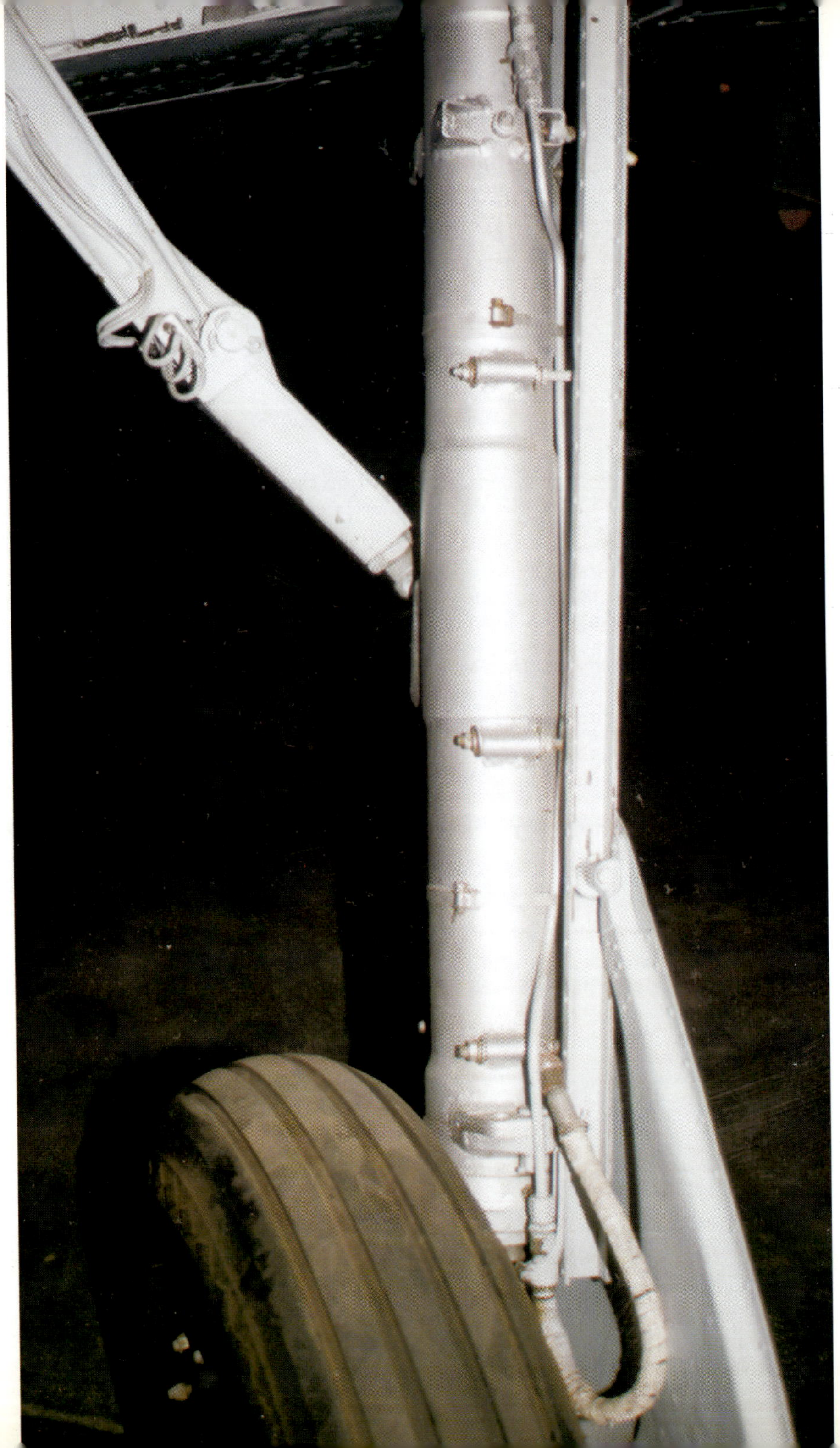

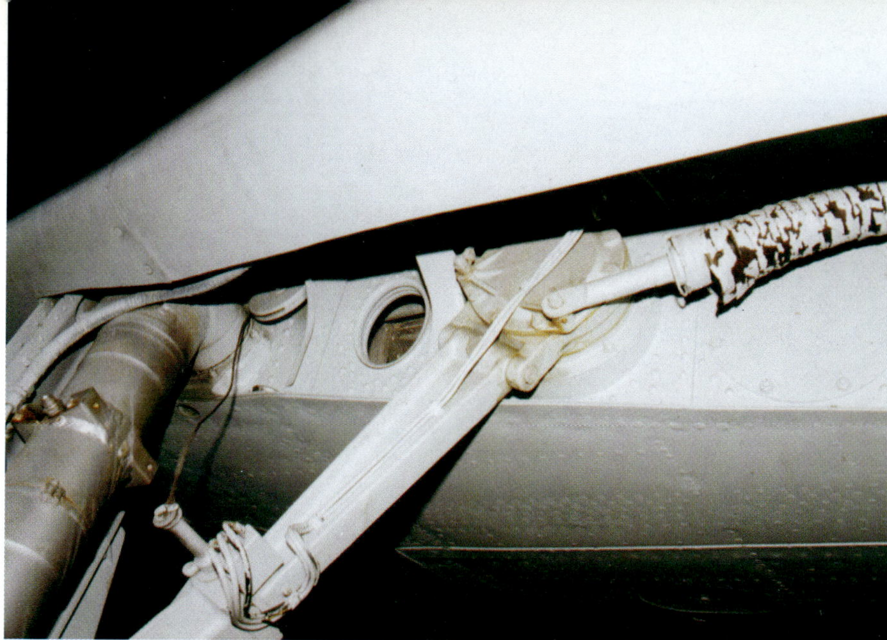

(Above) The upper radius rod of the starboard main gear and its attachment to the electric landing gear motor in the wing. Wiring for the microswitch on the bottom of the upper radius rod is attached. (Author: Ryle)

(Right) The starboard main landing gear's upper leg/wing 90 degree connection. This strut is late war type with welded leg features. The line on the strut is the top of the brake line. (Author: Ryle)

(Bottom Left) The rear of the starboard landing gear leg and linkage. Hanging from the bottom is the disconnected brake line. (Bottom Right) The lower front of the starboard landing gear. The brake line is attached to strut via small hose clamps — a common attachment method for brake and hydraulic lines. The piece extending outward from the bottom of the strut is the lower faring attachment outrigger. (Author: Ryle)

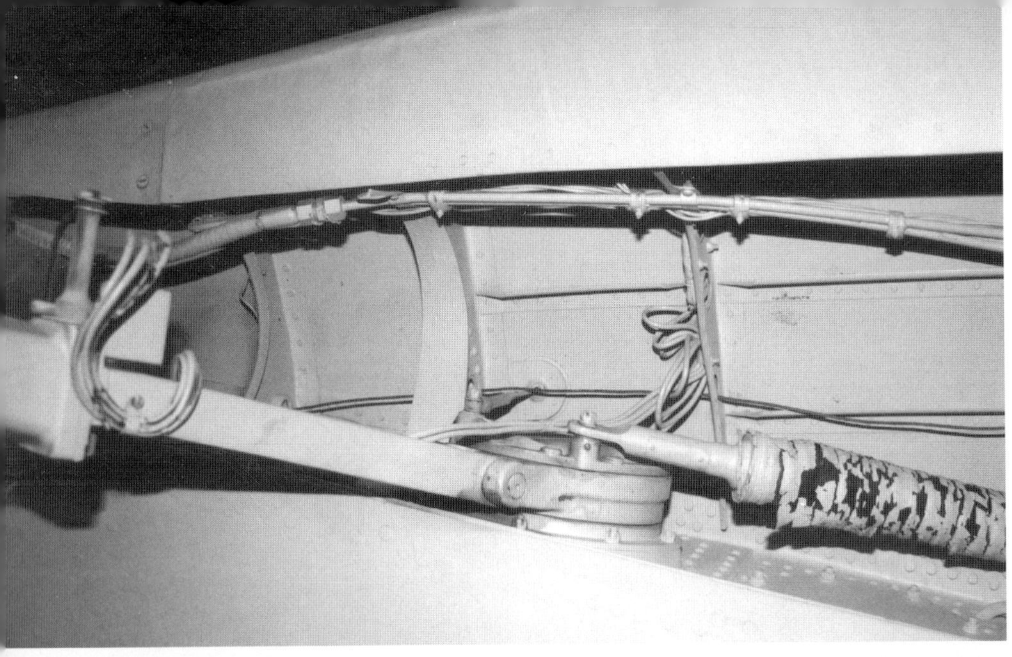

(Above) This photo shows the correct position of the electric gear drive, linkages and the strut.

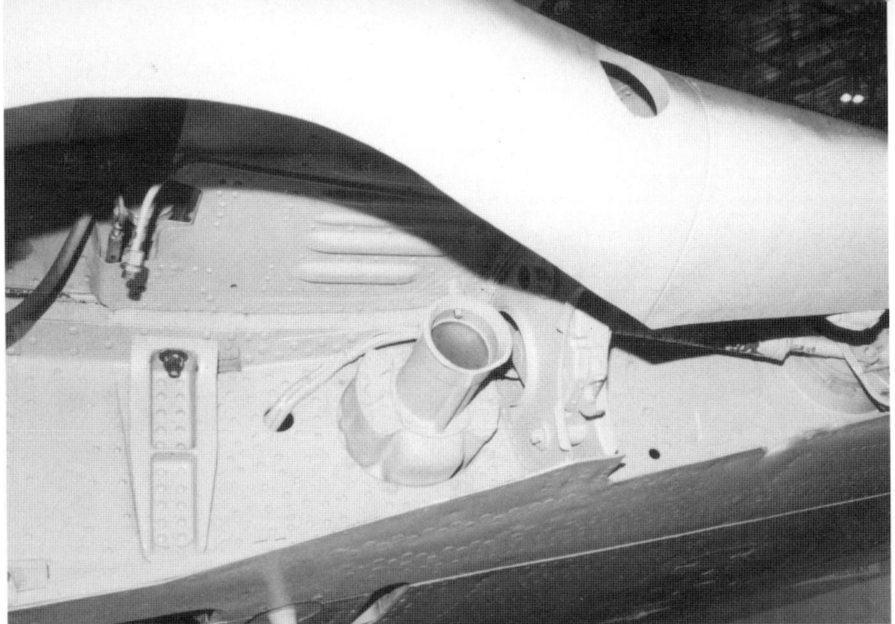

The right wing gun mount in the spar.

Landing Gear Operation

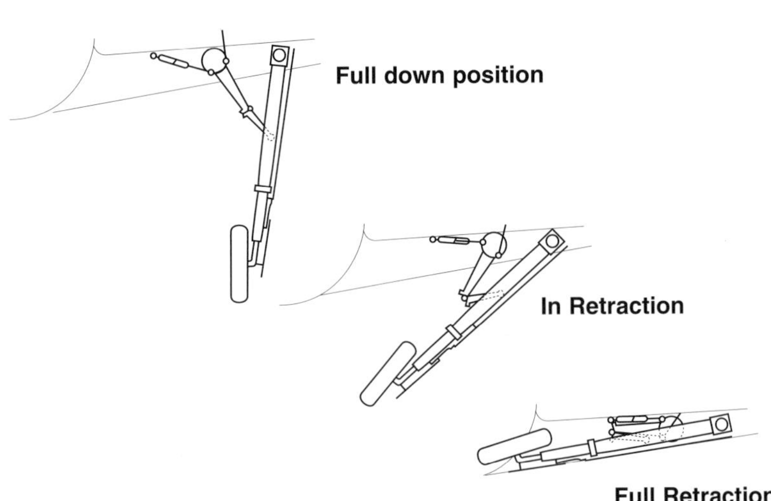

(Left) The tire on the NASM D-9 is an American made implement tire. The wheel is an unusual style and may be a replica since the tube filler indent is usually triangular in shape on the German made wheels. (Author: Ryle)

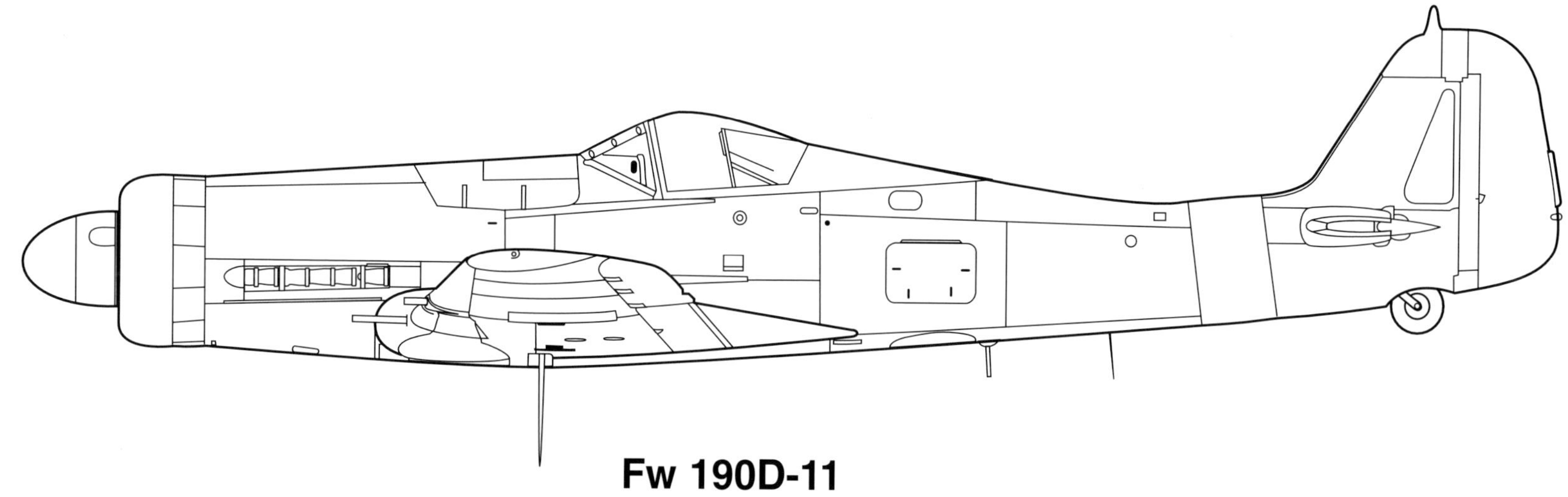

Fw 190D-11

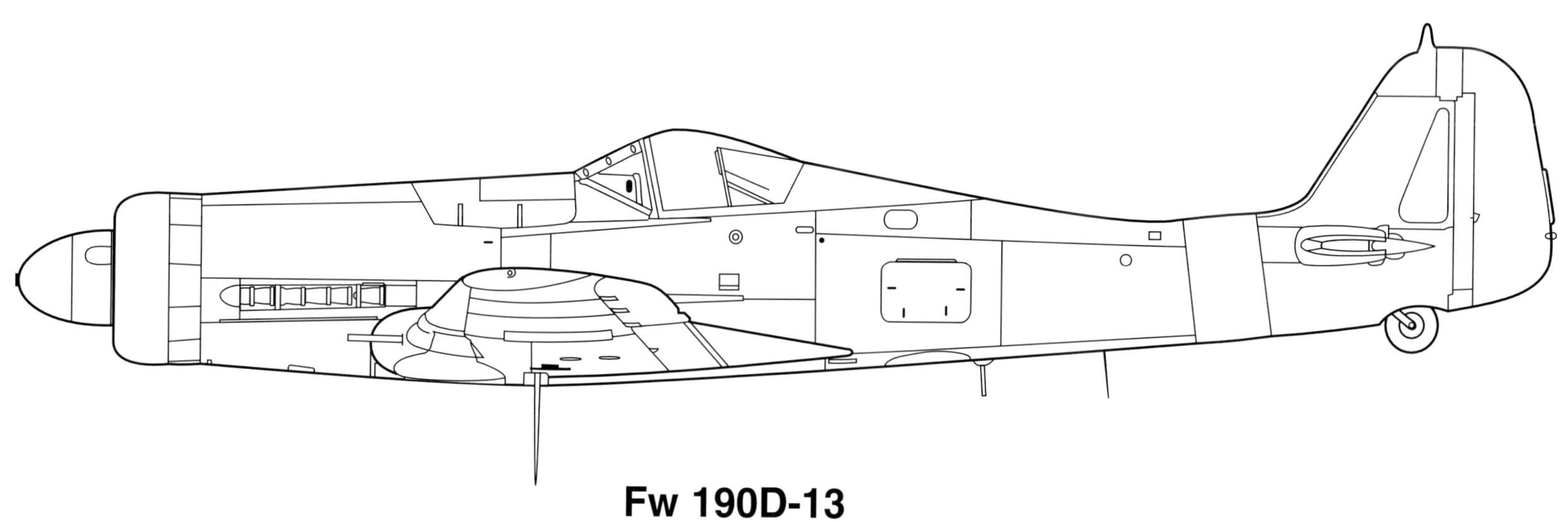

Fw 190D-13

(Above) The port side of the Champlin Fighter Aces Museum Fw 190D-13. It is believed that this was the 17th Fw 190D-13 manufactured. Built by Roland in March of 1945, the fuselage for this Fw 190D-13 was rebuilt from an Fw 190A-8 airframe (174013), which had been produced at the Focke-Wulf plant at Cottbus in May of 1944. This rebuilding of usable airframes was a common practice with Fw 190 production. (Author: Ryle)

PIK AS

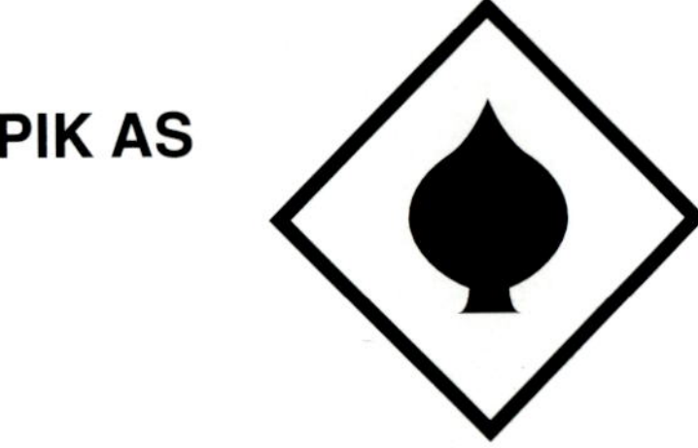

(Left) The supercharger intake on the starboard side of the engine compartment is a feature specific to the Fw 190D series, however the D-13 had a much larger and differently shaped supercharger intake than the D-9. (Author: Ryle)

The trailing edge of the horizontal stabilizer along with its connection to the elevator. The aircraft's Work Number (836017) is at the top of the vertical fin. The placement of the Work Number in this location was a standard practice throughout the war. (Author: Ryle)

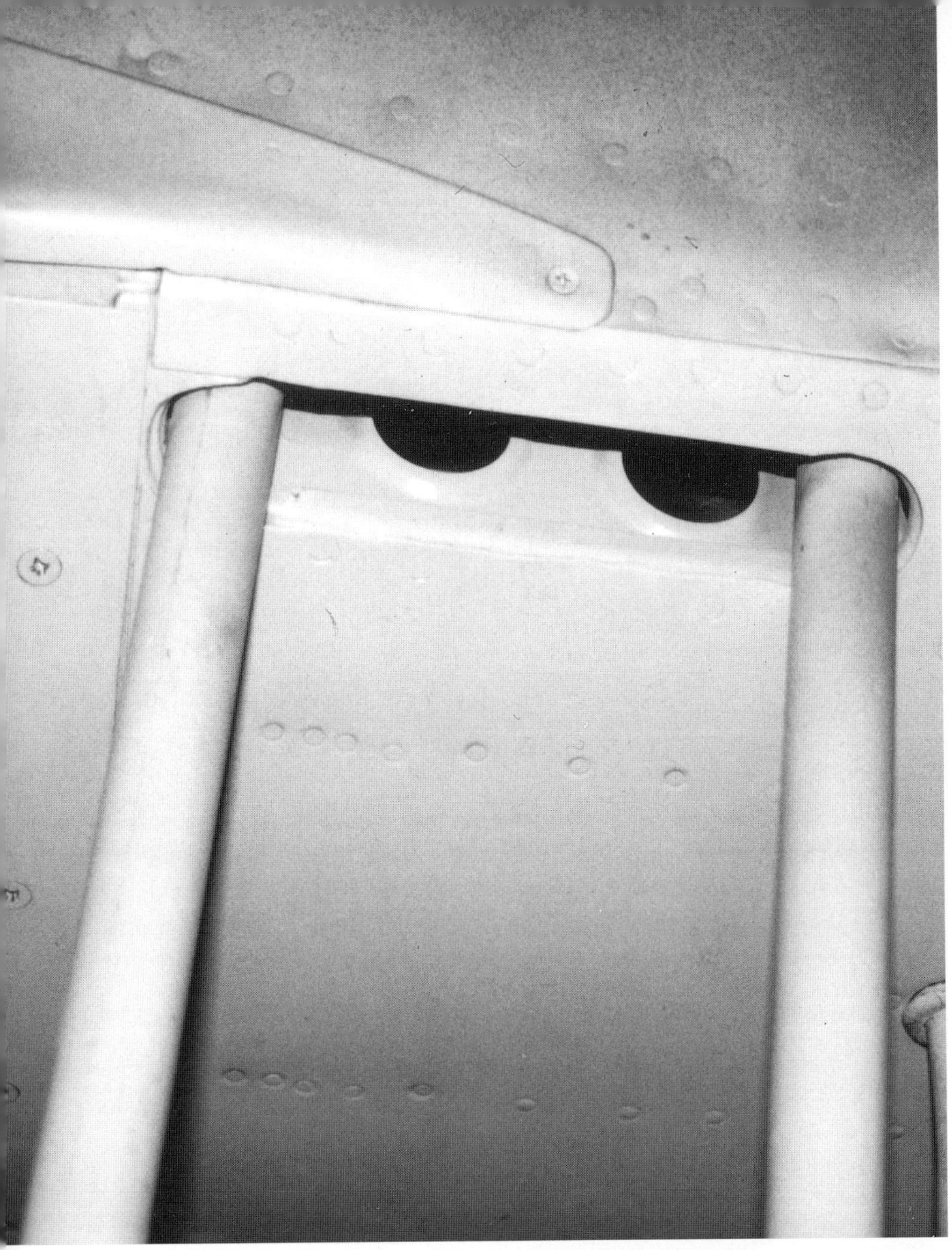

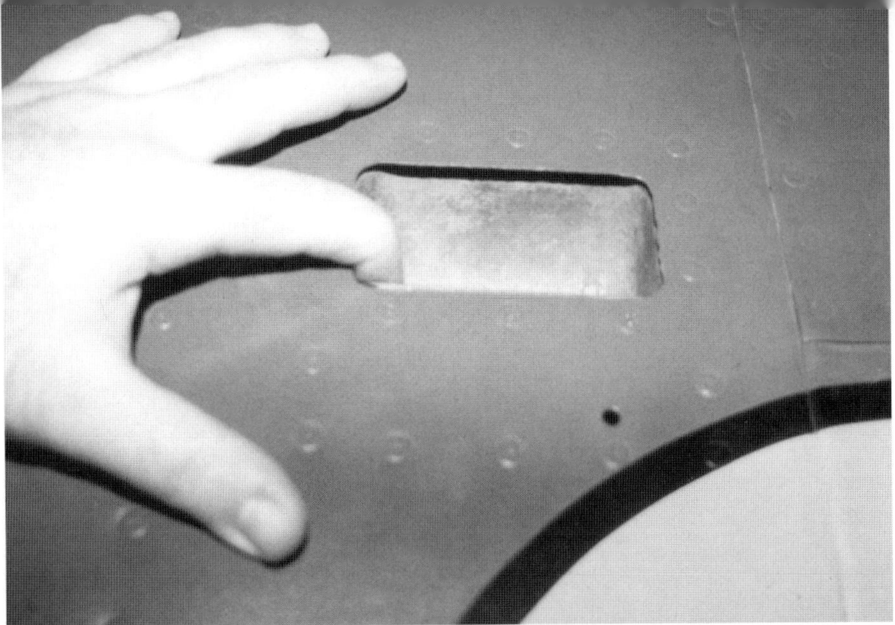

The pilot's hand grip on the port side of the fuselage is just above and forward of the Black outlined 'Yellow 0'. The small button on the top of the 'Yellow 0' is the button to release the droppable step. (Author: Ryle)

The pilot's foot step is located on the left side of the fuselage mid-way between the retractable foot step and the cockpit. The pilot would place his left foot in the step to assist his climb into the cockpit. (Author: Ryle)

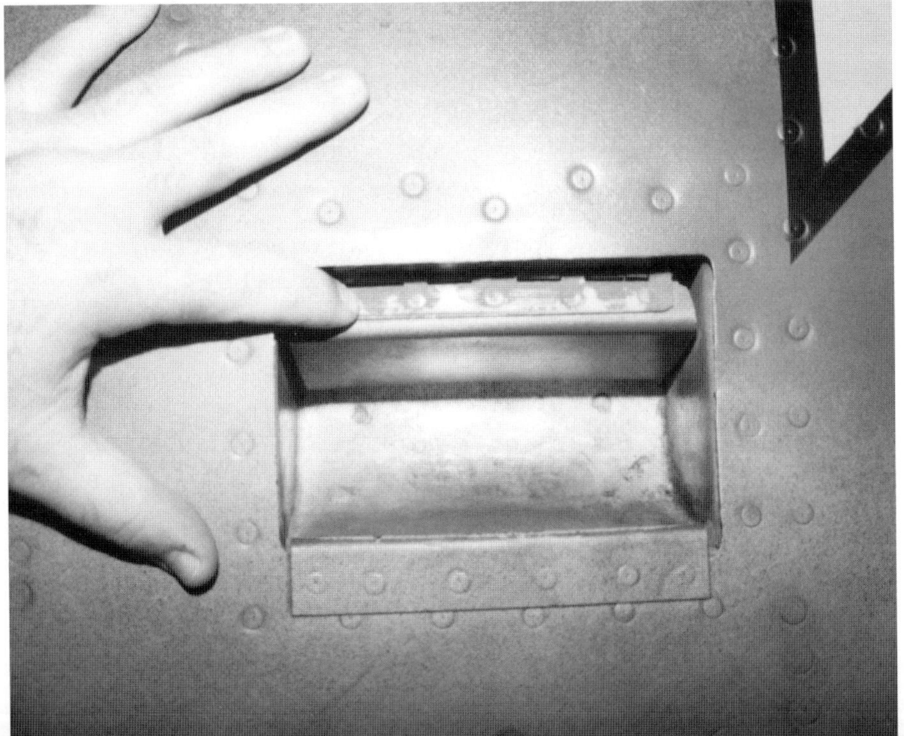

The pilot's extendible step on the port side of the fuselage. The two holes in the step's retraction trough are designed to both stiffen and lighten the step assembly. The small tube just to the right of the step is the auxiliary fuel tank overflow. In use, this tube may have been shorter than the one seen here. (Author: Ryle)

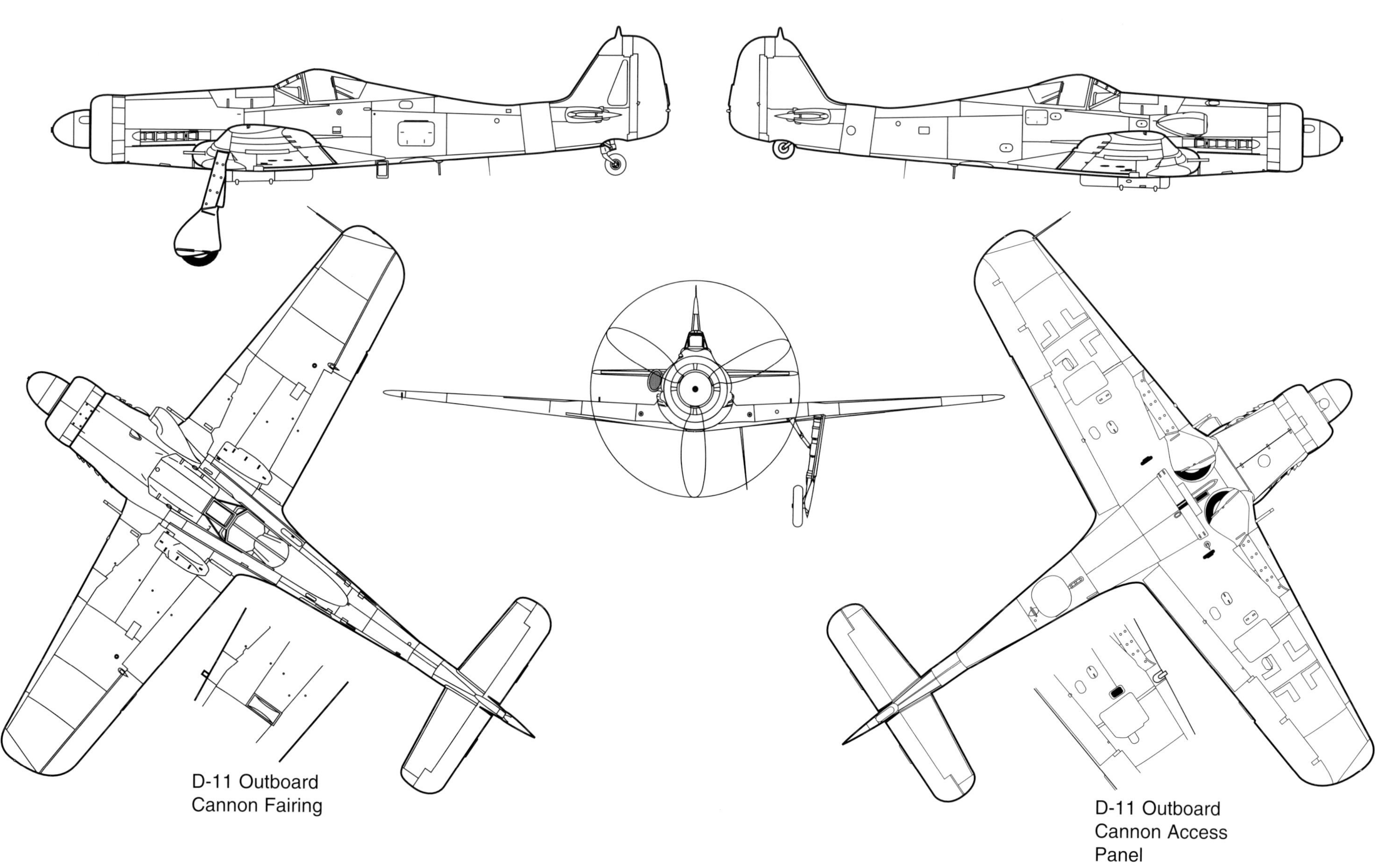

Focke-Wulf Fw 190D-13

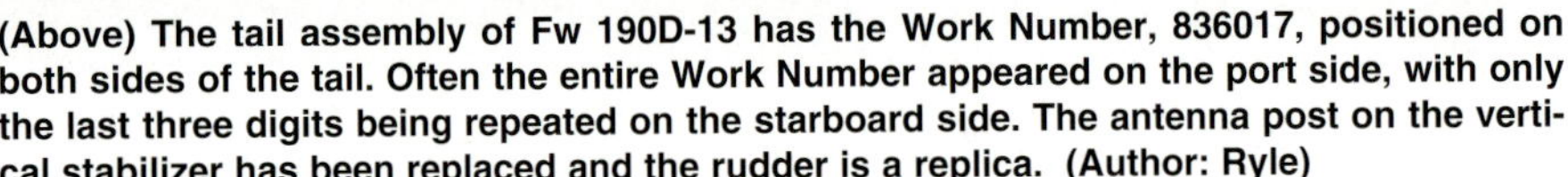

(Above) The tail assembly of Fw 190D-13 has the Work Number, 836017, positioned on both sides of the tail. Often the entire Work Number appeared on the port side, with only the last three digits being repeated on the starboard side. The antenna post on the vertical stabilizer has been replaced and the rudder is a replica. (Author: Ryle)

(Right) The replica rudder at full left deflection. The Fw 190 rudder had a cloth covering stitched to a heavy metal frame. The fixed metal trim tab is painted red. (Author: Ryle)

40

(Above and below) The replica horizontal stabilizer with the elevator in the full up and full down position. The horizontal stabilizer is all metal construction, while the elevator, like the rudder, is cloth over metal frame construction. The cloth is stitched to the elevator's frame, taped over, then the assembly is painted the same as the other parts of the aircraft. However, the difference in light reflection between the cloth covered parts and the metal parts almost made the fabric surfaces look like they were a different color. (Author: Ryle)

The + o - markings on the fuselage indicates the "horizontal stabilizer incidence" which could be adjusted by the pilot from +4 degrees to -1 degree, to compensate for changes in the aircraft's trim. A small electric motor in the tail actuated changes. The normal position is O (which is actually +2 degrees relative to the fuselage thrust line). (Author: Ryle)

The fuselage extension plug is painted with a Black and White Defense of the Reich band. The entry point of the vertical antennawire can be seen in the Black band. (Author: Ryle)

The small rectangular access panel on the port side of the fuselage in front of the vertical stabilizer allowed the ground crew to reach/check/tighten the bolts attaching the entire tail section to the fuselage. (Author: Ryle)

Looking aft, from the auxiliary fuel tank access door, this is the rod antenna for the FuG 25a IFF (Identify Friend/Foe), the fuselage extension plug, and one of the external stiffeners running from the rear of the plug to the tail wheel opening. (Author: Ryle)

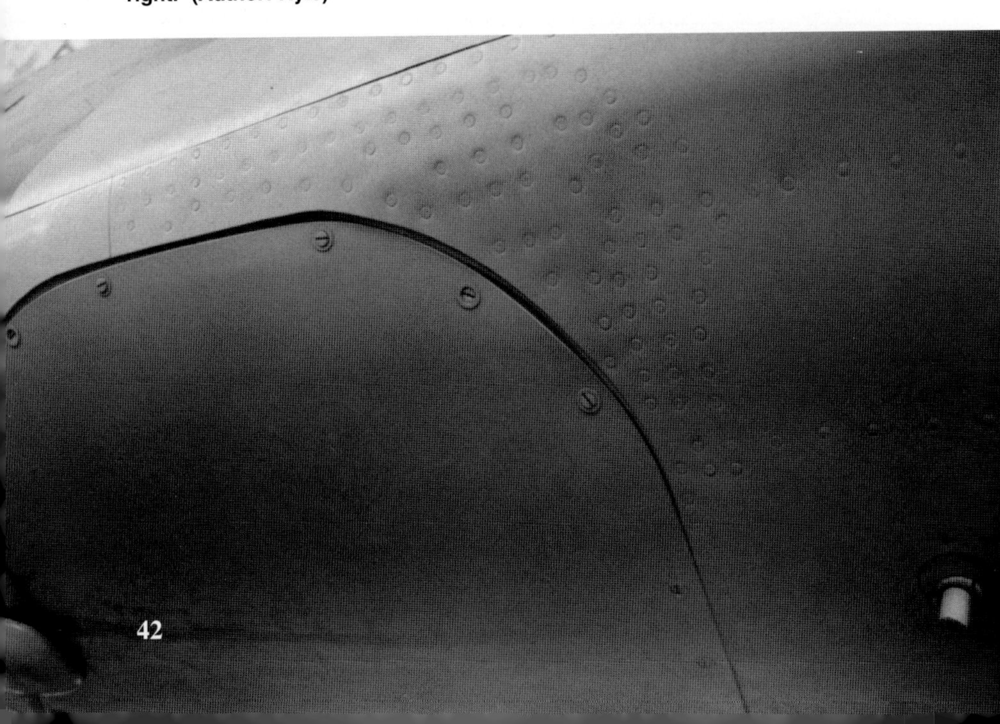

The bottom access panel to the auxiliary fuel tank. To conserve strategic resources late in the war this panel was made of wood. The main fuel overflow line may be seen on the right. (Author: Ryle)

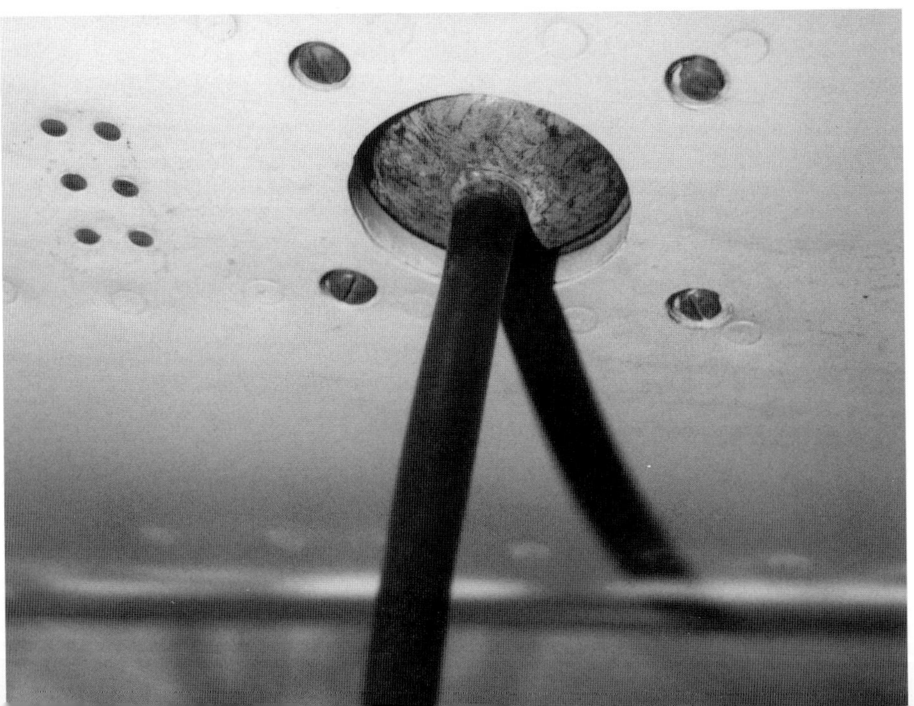

The attachment point of the FuG 25a IFF antenna mount. The brown material to which the rod antenna is attached is bakelite, a material of common use in German aircraft production. (Author: Ryle)

The external stiffener on the starboard side of the aircraft's fuselage. In the upper right is a fuel tank access panel with its yellow triangle. To the left is the "Pik-As" (Ace of Spades) emblem of JG 53 retained by this aircraft's last pilot, JG 26's last Kommodore, Major Franz Goetz. (Author: Ryle)

The starboard wing filet to the fuselage. The small panel with a bump in the center covers the bolt which attaches the wing to the fuselage. Aft of the attaching bolt is the front of an external stiffener common to Jumo 213 equipped long nose Fw 190s. (Author: Ryle)

The Tank/Focke Wulf engineering team did an excellent job in marrying the air-cooled BMW radial engined Fw 190A airframe to the Jumo liquid cooled in-line engine. The supercharger intake designed for late model Jumo 213 engine was larger than the intake on the D-9 series (This intake replaced the one installed during restoration and is now correct in appearance). (Author: Ryle)

The forward fuel tank filler door on the starboard side should have a centered opening latch, not a bottom latch as this one has. The flare tube is about a foot to the left of the access door and is covered with fabric to prevent hot exhaust gases from entering the cockpit; it can be identified by a slight discoloration in the paint. (Author: Ryle)

The starboard wing tip carried a Green navigation light. The angle of the pitot tube in relation to the angle of the wing is slightly downward. The tip of the pitot tube is not painted, but left in natural metal. (Author: Ryle)

(Right) The clean lines of the Fw 190 wing. On some Fw 190D upper wings had a bulge for the breech of an outboard 20mm cannon. This wing does not have an outboard cannon bulge and as such, could indicate that it was of late war manufacture. (Author: Ryle)

The red and white striped visual landing gear position indicator was on both wings. This small rod was attached to the main landing gear brace and protruded through the wing top of both wings when the gear was lowered, providing the pilot with a mechanical/visual indication that the landing gear was down. The attachment screws for the wing leading edge panels stand out along the wing panels. (author: Ryle)

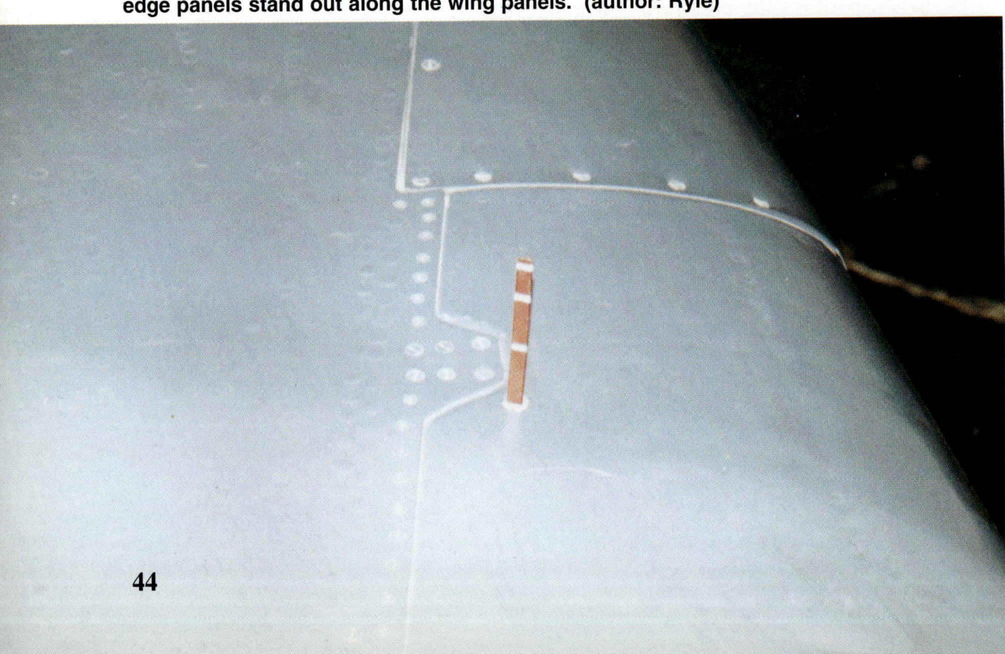

The starboard wing aileron in full up and in full down position. The aileron is cloth over a metal frame the same as the rudder and the elevators. Painted red, the metal trim tab is positioned quite close to the inboard edge of the aileron. (Author: Ryle)

The leading edge of the starboard wing has a small cover plate just outboard of the main gear which covers a hole originally intended for the MG FF 20mm cannon of an Fw 190A-0 through Fw 190A-5 aircraft. Since many Fw 190 wings were rebuilt and reused, these removable panels were used as fairings to cover the hole when the cannons were not fitted. (Author: Ryle)

The hole for installation of a 20mm or 30mm cannon barrel found intermitantly on Fw 190 A-6 through D-15 aircraft can be seen faired over just outboard of the landing gear. This cover panel is quite different from the one found on the starboard wing, and installation of either panel may have "occurred" at the factory or in the field. (Author: Ryle)

(Above) The lower starboard wing outboard trailing edge. The aileron is in the neutral position. The aileron's hinges at the wing can be seen as well as the cloth stitched over metal frame construction. (Author: Ryle)

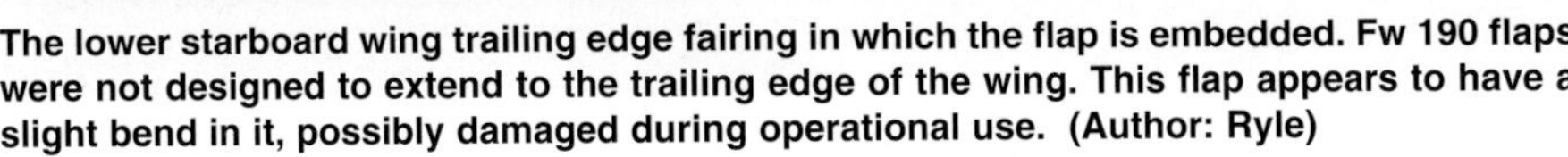

The lower starboard wing trailing edge fairing in which the flap is embedded. Fw 190 flaps were not designed to extend to the trailing edge of the wing. This flap appears to have a slight bend in it, possibly damaged during operational use. (Author: Ryle)

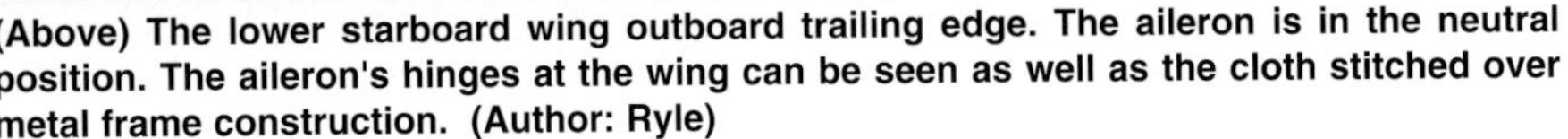

The Center aileron attachment bracket on the bottom of the wing. The small half moon cut-out in the aileron is to allow access to that part of the bracket. (Author: Ryle)

The inboard aileron attachment fitting on the bottom of the wing. The trailing edge of the wing and the leading edge of the aileron and bracket do not have a tight fit. This type of fit is not uncommon on Fw 190 wings. (Author: Ryle)

The flap pivot arm located on the leading edge in the center of the flap. The wing edge requires a small cut -out to allow clearance of the pivot when the flap is lowered. (Auhtor: Ryle)

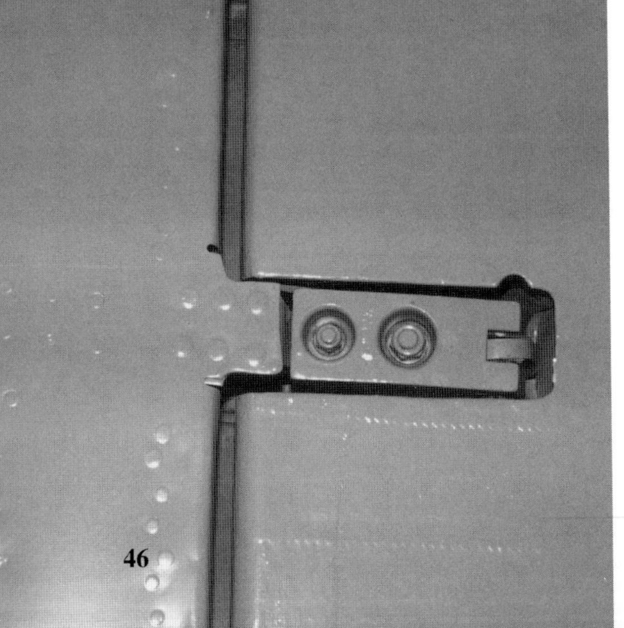

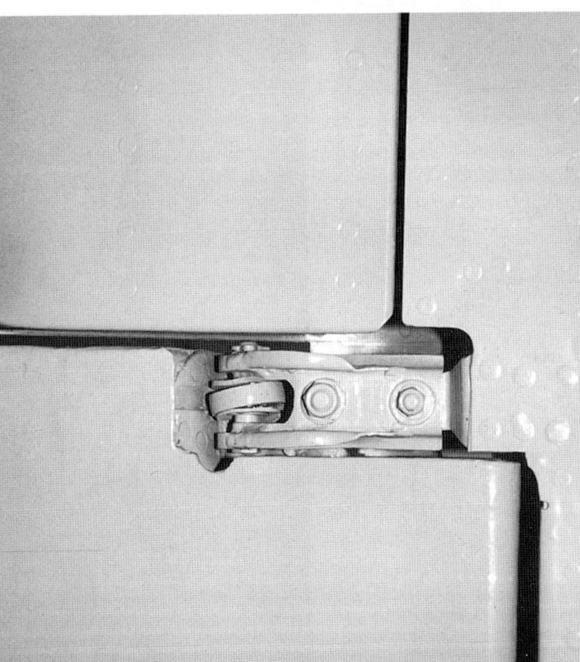

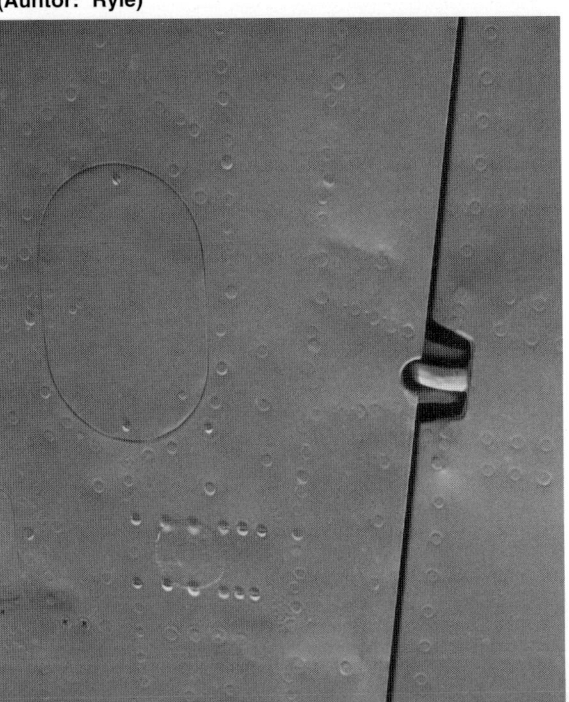

The lower outboard gun bay access panel on the starboard wing. These panels were originally used on the earlier Fw 190A to access the outboard wing mounted cannons. The outboard cannons were seldom installed on the Fw 190D, and this panel acted as a no more than a portion of the wing. (Author: Ryle)

(Left) The starboard wing flap is in the full up position and the aileron is in the full down position. The internal wing area behind the aileron is heavily reinforced with stiffeners. (Author: Ryle)

The lower starboard wing aileron in the full down position showing one of the attachment points of the aileron to the wing and some portions of the inner wing structure. (Author: Ryle)

(Above and above right) The port landing gear from the front and from the rear. The landing gear of the Fw 190 did not extend straight down from the wing, but with a very pronounced inward angle. The landing gear extend/retract arms (upper and lower radius rods) are not over-centered but appear to have a slight bend. The landing gear like the wheel well is painted RLM 02. (Author: Ryle)

The extend/retract arm's attachment to the rear of the EC-oleo shock strut on the port landing gear. The top of the scissors unit can be seen just above the wheel and immediately above that is the shock strut 'spur'. (Author: Ryle)

The starboard landing gear extend/retract arm. The wiring of the micro-switch may be seen as well as its plug-in on the rear wall of the wheel well. The tail wheel retract wire's attachment bolt is on the joint of the arm. (Author: Ryle)

With the starboard under carriage down the rear of the engine can be seen. The 20mm cannon barrel can be seen (without a barrel shroud installed) as well as the inboard inner wing structure and landing gear up-lock assembly. The tail wheel retract wire runs through the center length of the wheel well to a pulley at the edge of the engine area. The wheel well is painted RLM 02 Gray-Green. (Author: Ryle)

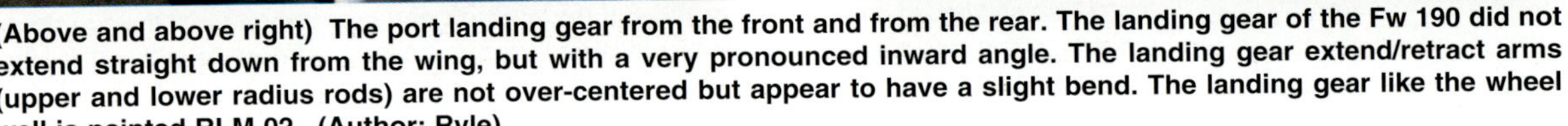

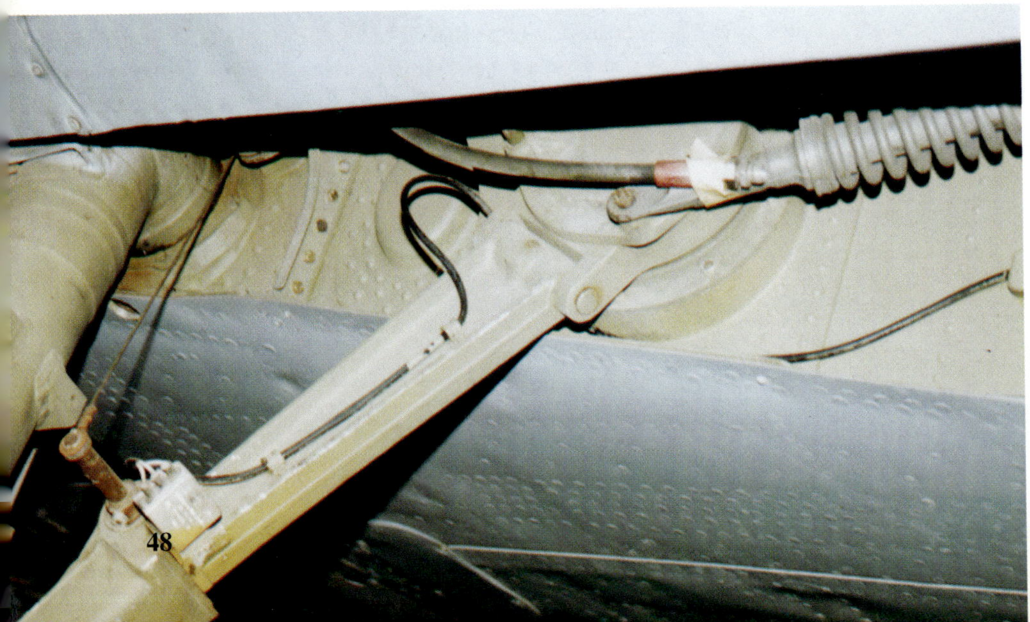

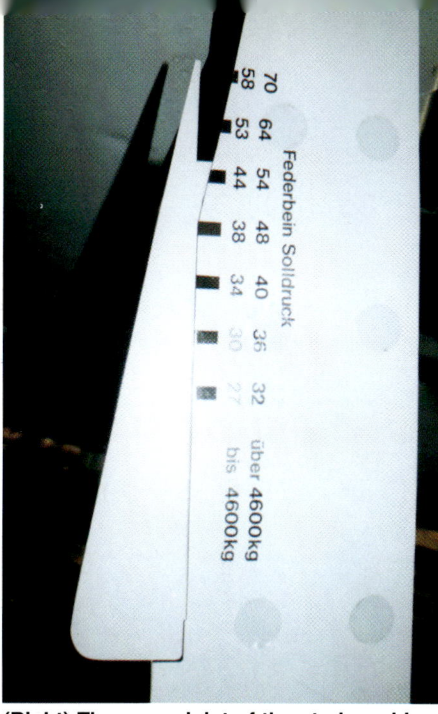

This late style wheel and tire are original. The wheel has a small yellow data tag between the red slip indicator and the tri-angular tire filler port. Most Fw 190 wheels were painted RLM 66 Black-Gray.

(Left) The stenciling on the (starboard) landing gear cover provides the proper main strut inflation for the take off weight. The small, round, darker blue areas are the cloth covers over the bolts securing the landing covers to the landing gear.

(Right) The upper joint of the starboard landing gear fits into the main spar by making a 90 degree bend toward the trailing edge of the wing. The wire attached to the upper extend/retract arm and the pulley in the corner of the wheel well is the tail wheel retract wire. This wire continues through the center of the wheel well to another pulley located beside the engine. (Author: Ryle)

(Below) The port landing gear rotating drive unit mounted at the rear of the wheel well in the main wing spar. On the other side of the spar inside the wing is an electric motor used to raise and lower the landing gear. The spring covered rod is the 'sealed air jack' used along with the force of gravity to lower the gear if the electric motor was not available.

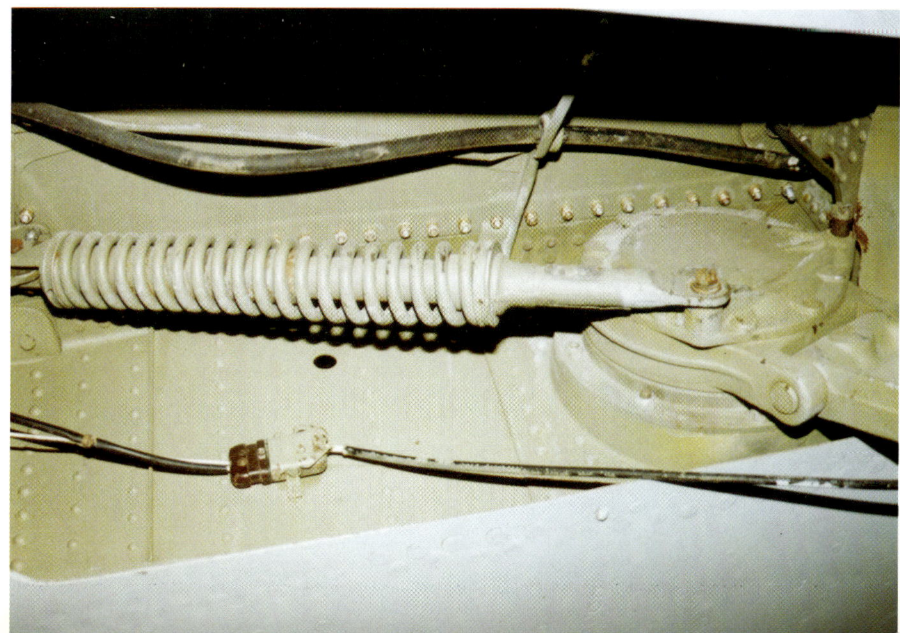

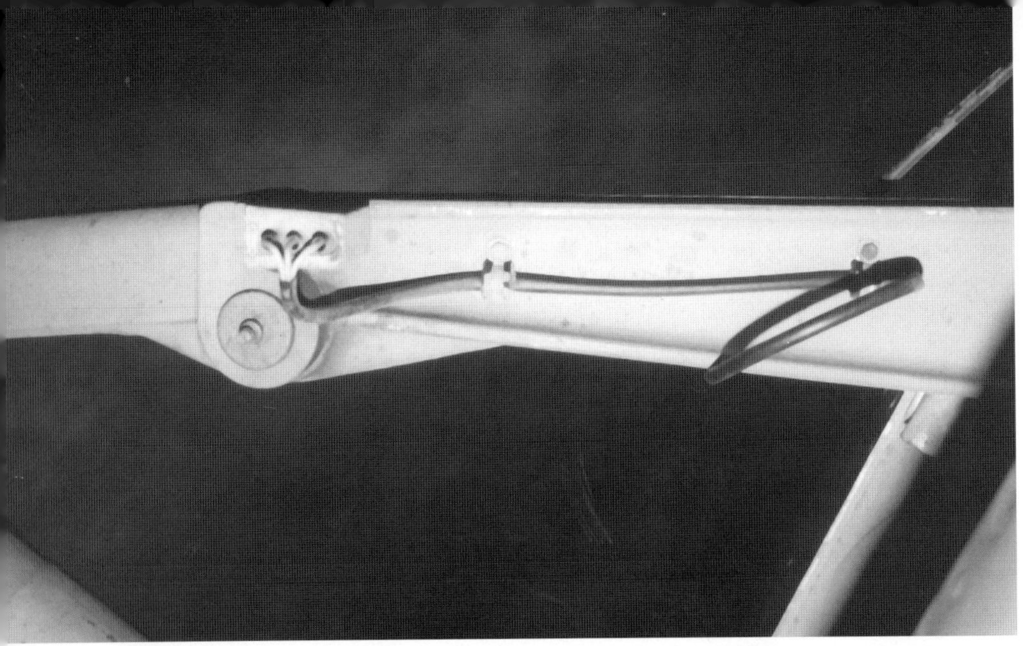

The front of the landing gear extend/retract arm on the port landing gear. The wiring on the upper arm is to the microswitch which actuated the cockpit landing gear down lock indicator and secured the landing gear drive motor. The wiring route shown here is incorrect for operational use since it would pinch against the wing skin when the gear is retracted. (Author: Ryle)

The landing gear up lock unit was both electric and manual, and secured the landing gear in the up position when the landing gear was retracted. The hook, in the open position, grabbed the shock strut spur on the rear of the landing gear oleo and pivoted to the closed position. (Author: Ryle)

MG 151 20mm Cannon

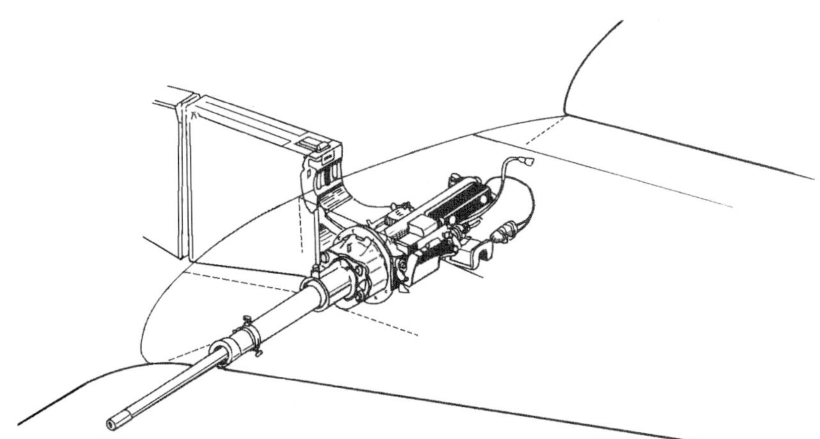

The port 20mm cannon, without a barrel shroud, coming through the upper wing spar. The main wing spar of the Fw 190 was a built up I-beam. The landing gear up-lock (locking unit) and hook for the shock strut spur is to the right of the cannon. (Author: Ryle)

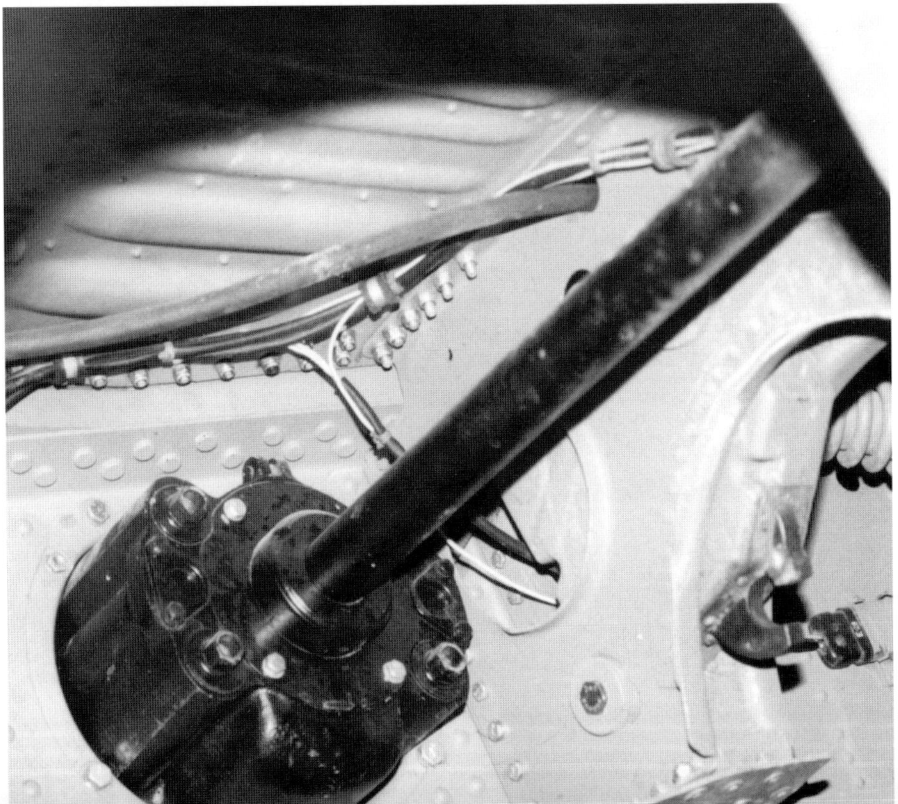

The inboard MG 151 20mm cannon and the gun camera port. The clear camera port was positioned slightly above the center line of the leading edge. No camera is fitted in the port, which was a common practice with Fw 190 aircraft. (Author: Ryle)

The disposal cartridge and link chute for the inboard wing mounted MG151 20mm cannon. The small hole aft of the chute opening was used to access the mounting screw for the internally fitted chute (which has been removed in this photo). (Author: Ryle)

Wing Root 20mm Cannon Ejection Chutes

The port wheel well. The main wing spar serves as the rear wall of the wheel well, with the 20mm cannon mounting extending through the spar. The landing gear up-lock is to the right of the 20mm cannon barrel. Various wiring and a plug-in for the landing gear cockpit indicators run along the wing spar. (Author: Ryle)

The red cross in a white circle identifies the medical stowage door. Through the open cockpit the instrument panel can be seen. The white padding around the instrument panel is non-standard, however, padding was installed in a darker color. (Author: Ryle)

The control stick and its lower assembly, without the leather boot installed. The arm extending from the right side of the assembly (a replacement added during restoration), controls the elevators. On the bottom of the left side console is a small, bent rod which functioned as the throttle lever friction control. This was also added during restoration. Normally, a grooved, 2" diameter rod was used for this purpose. (Author: Ryle)

The left lower instrument panel is a replica with some original instruments installed. The KG13B stick grip with its data tag can be seen. (Author: Ryle)

Two different styles of original rudder pedals are installed, which were usually installed in like pairs, however with the continuous re-building of damaged machines this configuration could easily have happened. Behind the instrument vacum flask is the fire wall with a Black metal plate covering the hole where the 20mm cannon's breech protruded into the cockpit. (Author: Ryle)

This instrument panel is not standard for an Fw 190D-9, but it's configuration is within the variations seen on late war variant of the Fw 190D. The cockpit, including the instrument panel, would normally have been painted RLM 66 Black-Gray which is not as dark as the paint seen here. (Author: Ryle)

The seat belts are original. The seat bottom usually contained a cushion. The step on the rear of the seat is to support the pilot's back pack parachute. The seat would have been painted RLM 66 Black Gray. (Author: Ryle)

The 'oxygen group' of gauges, in blue on the lower instrument panel, are in front of the combat clock, which is mounted horizontally, on the forward portion of the right console. (Author: Ryle)

The right side of the replica lower panel. The only original part of the panel is the clock, which is located at the very front of the panel. The crank on the side wall is to open and close the canopy. The white square is the canopy eject lever, normally painted red. (Author: Ryle)

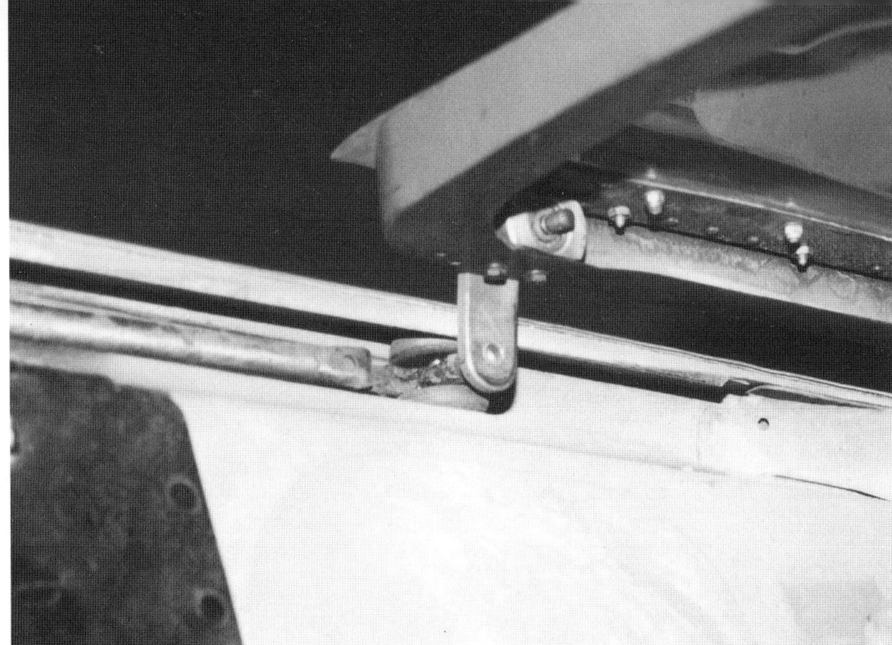

(Above and below) The pilot's view through the Revi 12 gun sight and a side view of the Revi 12. The thickness of the armored glass in the windscreen can be seen. The sight is mounted to the right of centerline on the instrument panel shield. However, during the period of the war that the Fw 190D-13 operated, the gun sight installed would probably have been a Revi 16d. (Author: Ryle)

With the canopy moved to fully open the tracks and rollers that the canopy slides on can be seen on either side of the fuselage. The canopy roller assembly seen here was added during restoration and is non-standard. The canopy track has an upward slope at the rear of the track to insure that if the canopy was jettisoned it left completely and smoothly. (Author: Ryle)

Revi 12 Gunsight

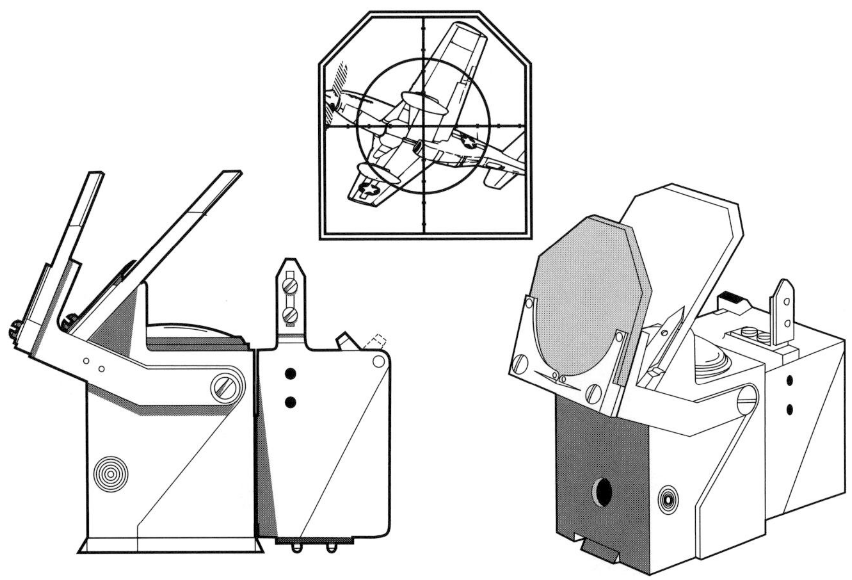

The general shape and of this two-piece replica 'blown hood' canopy and headrest is very close to the original. The antenna wire connects to the outside of the canopy above the headrest and does not enter the blown hood. The only entry of the antenna into the fuselage is the vertical wire's connection at the rear of the fuselage spine. (Author: Ryle)

When the blown hood canopy is in the closed position the antenna wire is pulled taught. The original flat canopies were one piece clear Plexiglas with a hinge line cut into the forward, upper clear area. The two-piece 'Blown Hood' canopy was far easier to manufacture and repair than the earlier one piece flat hood.   (Author: Ryle)

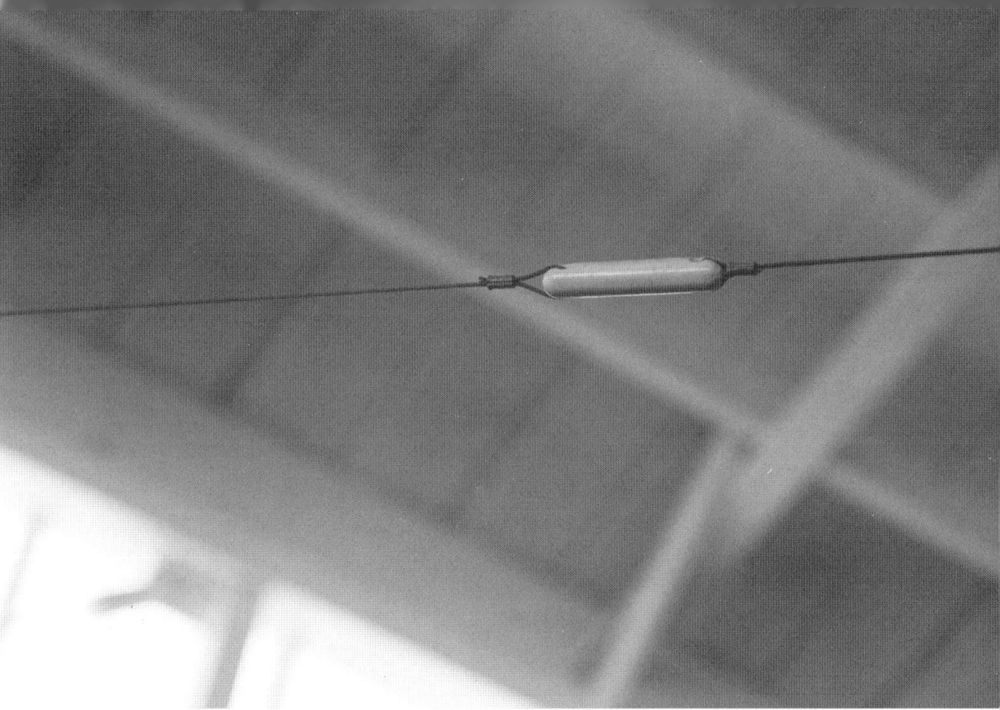

(Above and below) The connection of the vertical antenna wire that runs from the aircraft's spine to the main antenna wire running from the canopy to the top of the tail. Resistors are located on the main wire on either side of the vertical antenna wire. The wire is a correct bronze color. (Author: Ryle)

The hole in the center of the spinner is for the engine mounted 20mm cannon that fired through the propeller hub. The additional cannon provided the Fw 190D-13 with much needed firepower, but this arrangement gave problems and some aircraft are reported to have flown without the engine mounted cannon installed. (Author: Ryle)

The first exhaust pipe is partially covered by an aerodynamic faring and above the three exhausts in the center is a small fairing designed to keep the exhaust gases out of the supercharger air intake. (Author: Ryle)

The Fw 190D-13 used a Junkers VS 10 variable pitch propeller. The blade seen here maybe original (but possibly not a VS 10), and if so, could have been made from one piece of hard wood with a metal leading edge and an exterior of painted cloth. The wrinkle lines on the blade are the result of the wooden blade shrinking inside its cloth cover. (Author: Ryle)

The spinner's back plate was attached to the spinner with a number of small screws. The opening for the radiator was quite small with a vast amount of the nose section being occupied by the large bulbous spinner. (Author: Ryle)

Just behind and under the cowl flaps, the fuselage can be seen to taper providing for air flow through the nose mounted radial radiator. (Author: Ryle)

(Above and below) The size and shape of the later model intake found on the Fw 190D-11/12/13 and Ta 152 is much larger than the intake found on the earlier Fw 190D-9. The intake did not lie against the fuselage side and was made by welding together several component pieces. (Author: Ryle)

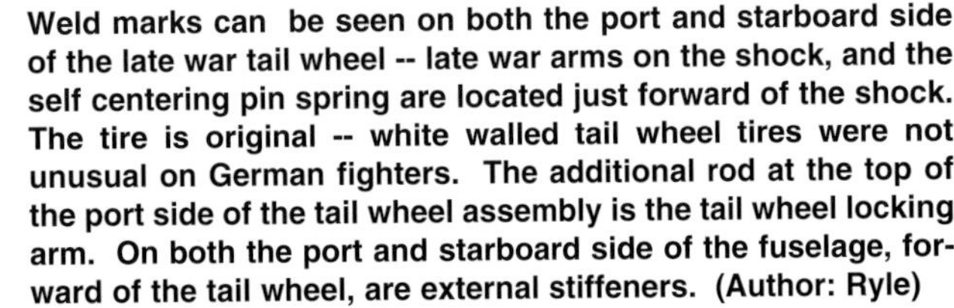

Weld marks can be seen on both the port and starboard side of the late war tail wheel -- late war arms on the shock, and the self centering pin spring are located just forward of the shock. The tire is original -- white walled tail wheel tires were not unusual on German fighters. The additional rod at the top of the port side of the tail wheel assembly is the tail wheel locking arm. On both the port and starboard side of the fuselage, forward of the tail wheel, are external stiffeners. (Author: Ryle)

(Above) With the cowl flaps open the actuator rods pushing out the interconnected cowling flaps can be seen. (Author: Ryle)

(Below) The black hose connected to the bottom rear of the radiator is the lower coolant line. (Author: Ryle)

Although no cowling armament was carried, the cowling gun bay cover was retained. The hole for the external starter and the small intake for the pilot's cockpit cooling air can be seen. The engind panels must bulge outward to cover the Ta 152 type engined mounts of the Jumo 213 engine. The cowl flaps do not run across the top of the engine since this would have further obstructed the pilot's already limited forward view. (Author: Ryle)

The upper engine cowling with panels open. The attachment of the motor mount was via the upper engine bearer links to the fuselage. The 'links' were required to fit the late model Jumo engine, with Ta 152 motor mounts, into the Fw 190D airframe. The open area in the center was occupied by 13mm cowling machine guns on Fw 190D-9 aircraft. The rear of this machine gun area, the windscreen mount, does not have the access holes found on Fw 190A/F/G aircraft. (Author: Laing via Goss)

The engine compartment panels fold upward on each side, while the gun panel opens aft and lays flat against the armored windscreen. With no room to spare it is easy to see why the upper engine bearer links must bend downward to attach to the fuselage. (Author: Laing via Goss)

(Right) Looking directly down into the rear of the engine compartment at the fire wall. The upper engine bearer link bends slightly outward to attach to the fuselage brackets. The taped over pilot's air intake is on the fire wall to the left of the silver supercharger which has the generator partially overlapping it. Just above the pilots air intake on the fire wall is the silver box containing the ignition relay. The yellow coolant tank is just above the silver oil tank. The starboard engine bearer curves slightly outward to meet the fuselage attachment. (Author: Laing via Goss)

The lower port side motor mount passes through the oil tank to secure itself to the lower left side of the fuselage. (Author: Laing via Goss)

The starboard side of the engine/fire wall area, just behind the super charger intake. The Black/Silver/Black cylinder above the supercharger is the generator. (Author: Laing via Goss)

The starboard side of the engine looking at the supercharger; the white tank to the right is a coolant tank. (Author: Laing via Goss)

The bottom engine panels are opened providing a view of the under side of the engine from front to back. In the center are the fuel injectors, ignition harness and fuel lines. (Author: Ryle)

Fw 190D Canopy and Aerial

Flat Hood

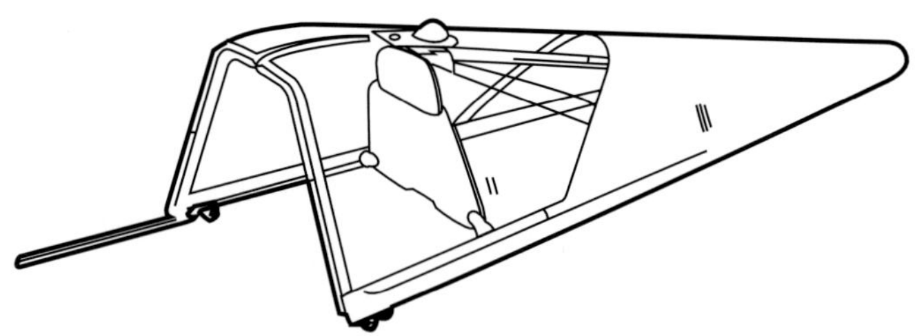

Blown Hood

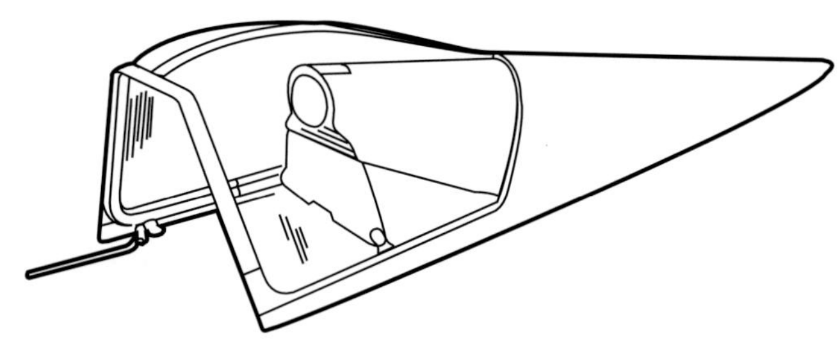

The two types of Fw 190 cockpit canopies. The top canopy is the early, flat style with which most Fw 190Ds left the factory. This canopy has a piano hinge at its top front to allow flexing inward without breaking when the canopy is opened and the canopy's front rollers move inward within the narrowing fuselage canopy rails. The later style, blown hood canopy is made in two pieces joined at the top via a single strip of bracing. This was a simpler construction technique providing more room and visibility while still allowing the canopy to flex on opening without breaking.

Flat Hood — closed

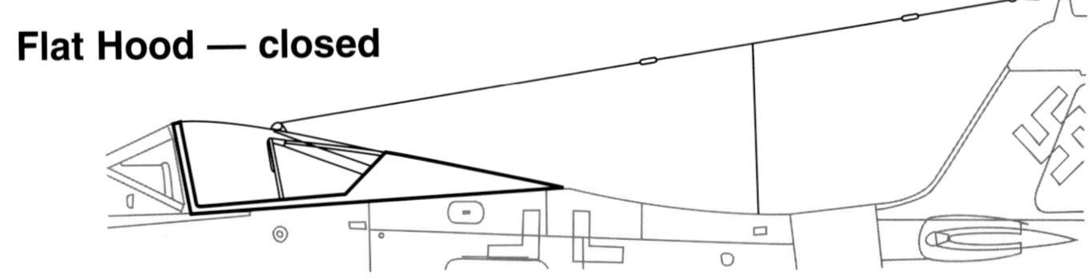

Flat Hood — open

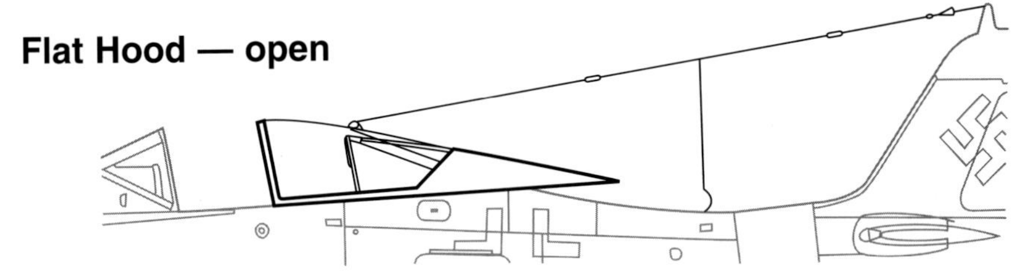

Blown Hood — closed

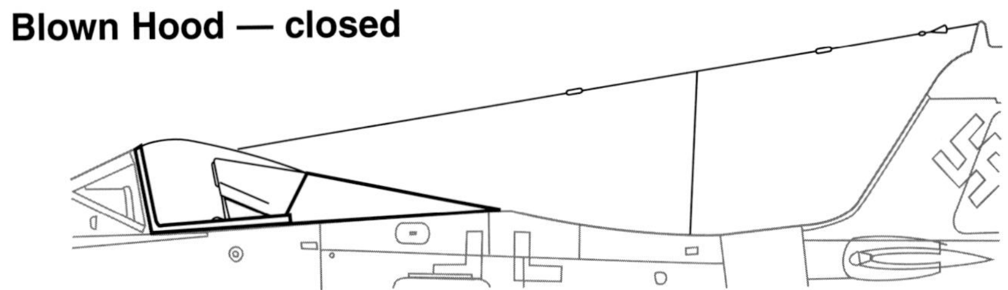

Blown Hood — open

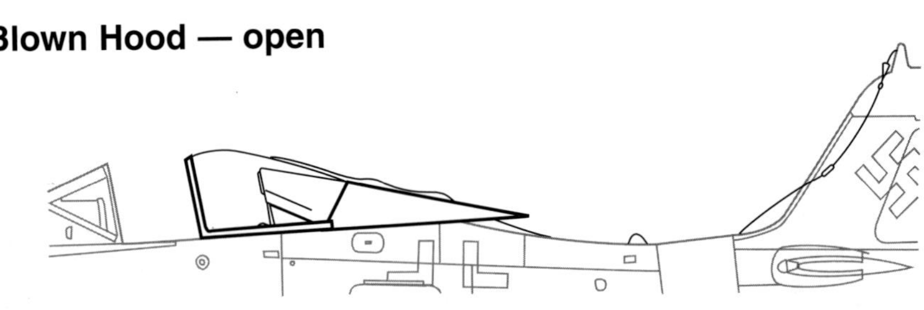

(Above) The canopy jettison tube can be seen under the metal portion of the canopy extending over the fuselage spine. With the canopy open, the antenna wire has dropped to the fuselage side. A drooped antenna wire with an open 'blown hood' is correct for an operational Fw 190. (Author: Ryle)

The canopy was jettisoned via rearward pressure on this tube by a 28mm (blank flare gun) explosive charge located behind the pilot's seat. The tube's opening is located in the middle of the fuselage and the fuselage spine seam is offset to starboard. This offset is correct for all Fw 190 fuselage and may be to either side of the spine's center. (Author: Ryle)

The pilot's view out of the cockpit was good above and to the sides but the forward view was limited. The very low angle of the armored windscreen and it's small size restricted forward visibility. (Author: Ryle)

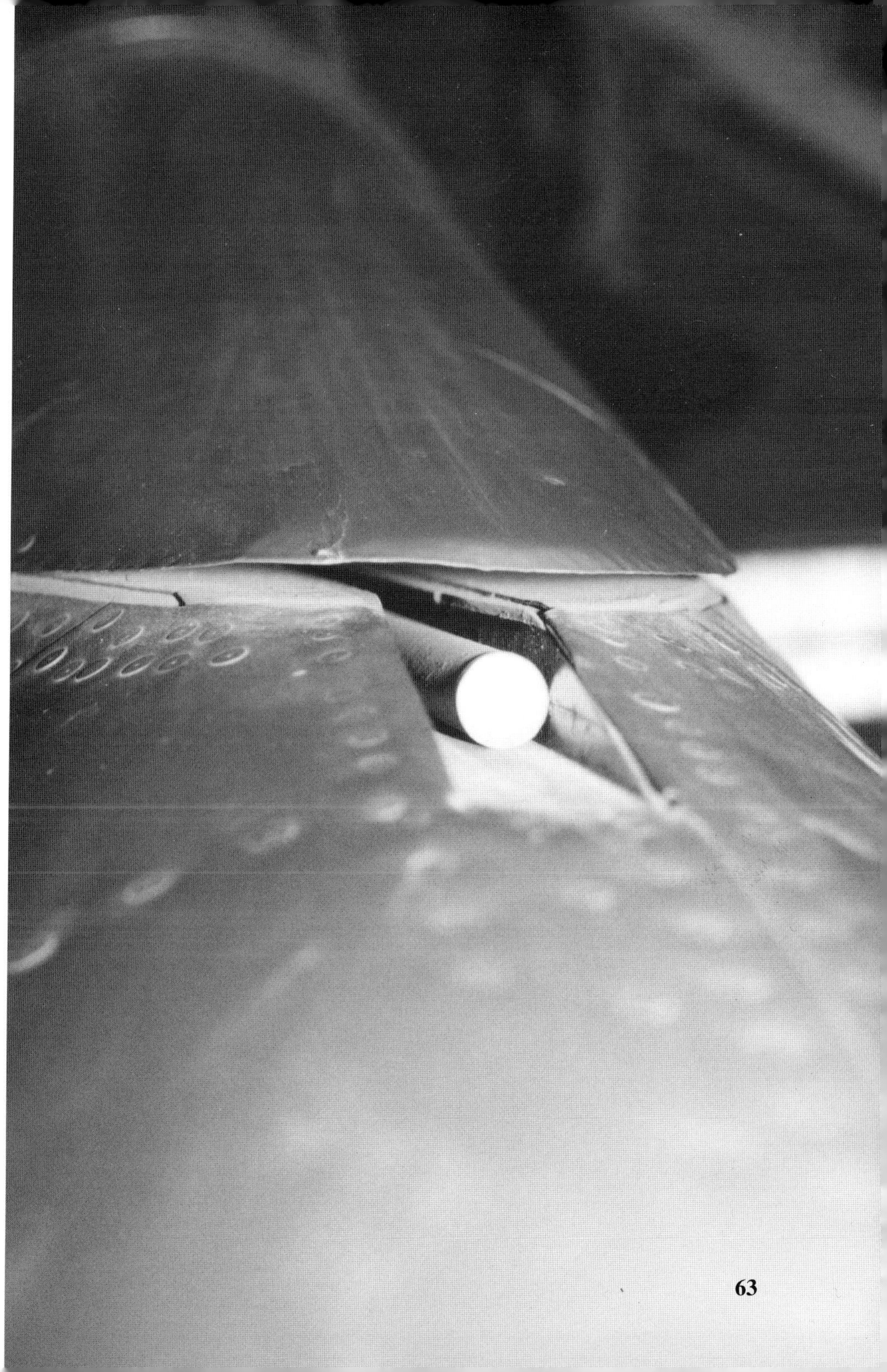

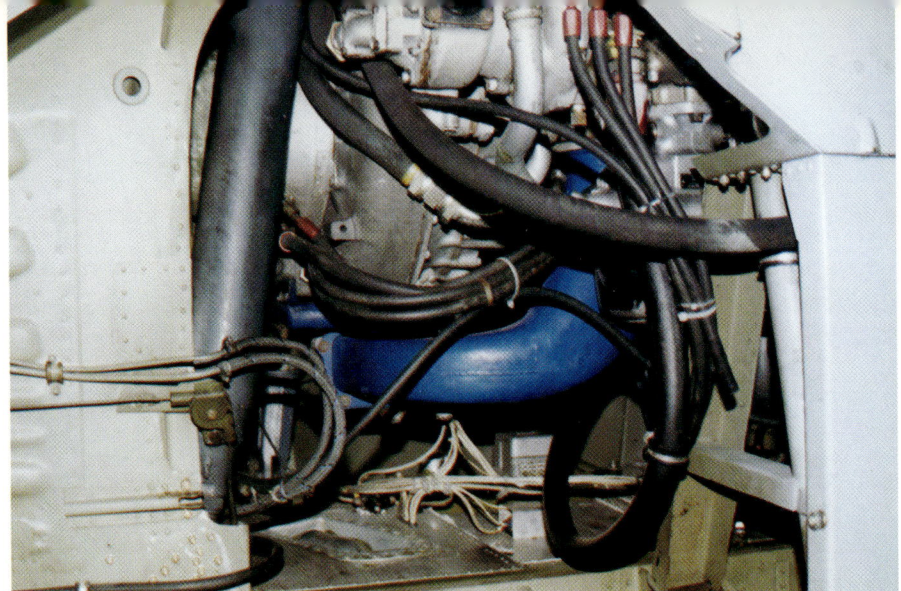

The two raised sections in front of the wheel well are a design feature left over from the radial engine of the Fw 190A series which served to channel the exhaust from the lower exhaust bank of the BMW 801 radial engine. A smooth panel for this area was designed for the D series aircraft, but since the wings of the Fw 190 A and D were the same, and the parts interchangeable, this rebuilt A series wing retained this feature. The wing installed on this aircraft was not the wing used operationally by this aircraft. (Author: Ryle)

A cowl latch was on the top of cowl. The cowl flaps which had an extremely close fit were opened to provide additional cooling to the engine. (Author: Ryle)

The starboard wheel well. The dimpled patterned wheel well center panels used on the earlier Fw 190A series were not retained on the Fw 190D — the mass of hoses and wiring at the aft end of the Jumo 213 engine can be seen where these panels were removed. The gray steel tube on the left of the engine opening is the motor mount. (Author: Ryle)

The port wheel well. The large tank to the right of all the plumbing is the engine oil reservoir. To the left, the bracing frame between the two wheel wells (painted RLM 02) was originally designed to help support the BMW 801 radial engine on earlier Fw 190A aircraft and was retained on the Fw 190D. (Author: Ryle)

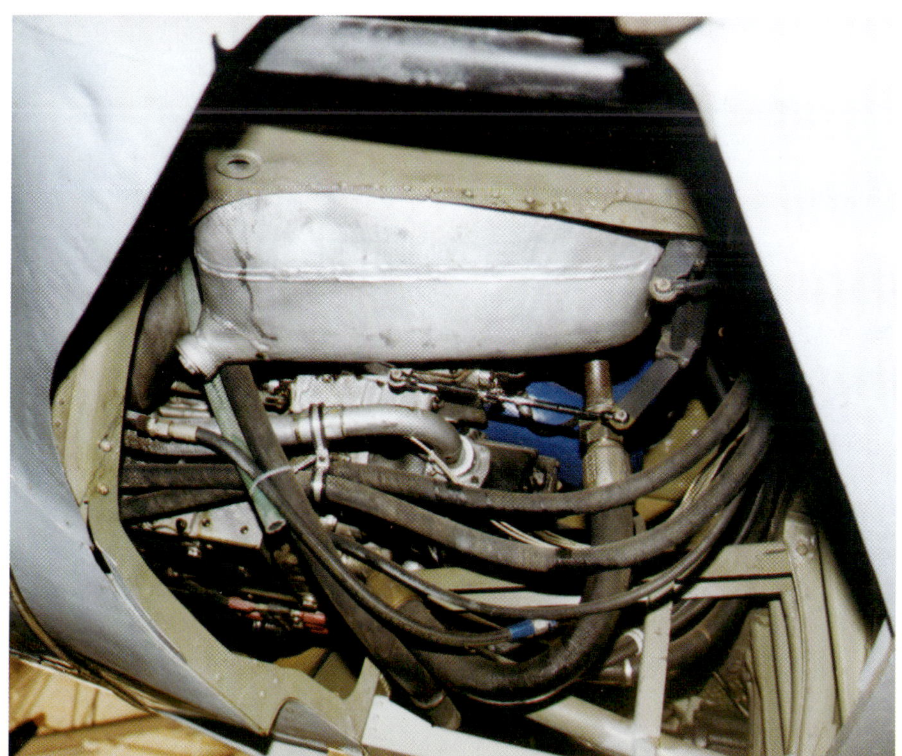

(Above and below) The additional space required to mate the Jumo 213 engine to the Fw 190D airframe was the reason the center wheel well panels could not be installed: The Jumo 213 engine and its additional plumbing required the forward and upper portion of the wheel well center. The supercharger installed on the liquid cooled Jumo in-line engine also requred additional room. (Author: Ryle)

The Yellow 115 liter auxiliary fuel tank was used for either fuel or methanol for the MW 50 power booster. The elevator control cables run along the starboard side of the fuselage. (Author: Ryle)

Looking at the floor of the fuselage through the port side, this machine has a metal auxiliary fuel tank access door frame. The bracket in the center of the photo is a battery holder added during restoration. (Author: Ryle)

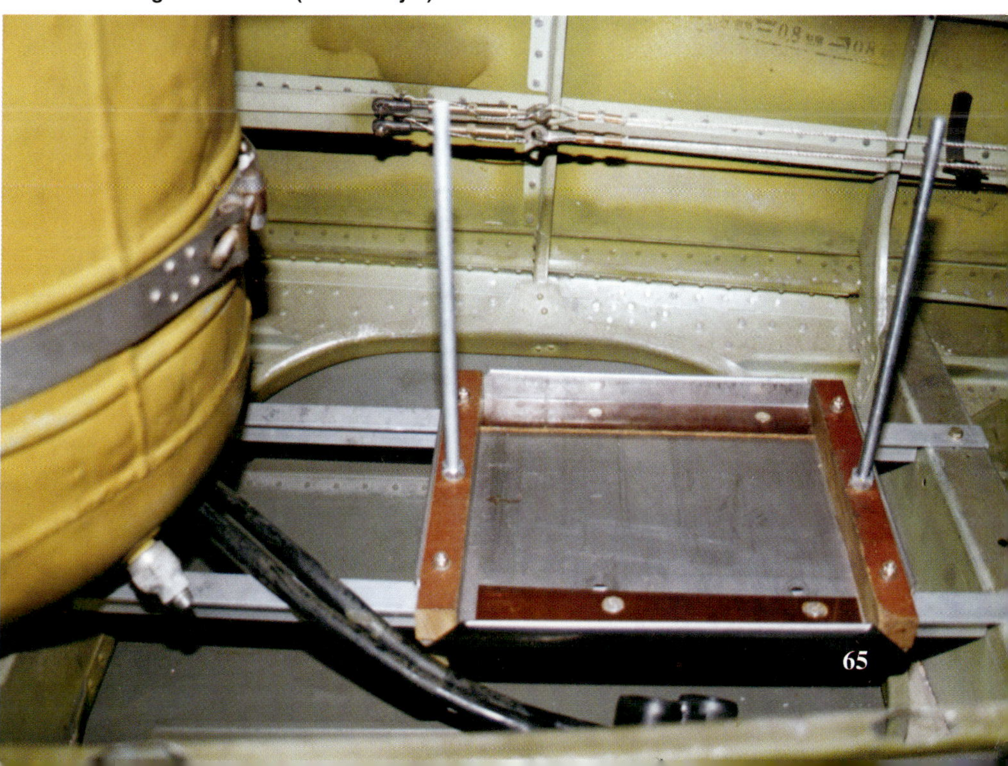

Additional or redesigned areas of the Fw 190A airframe required for the Fw 190D series aircraft.

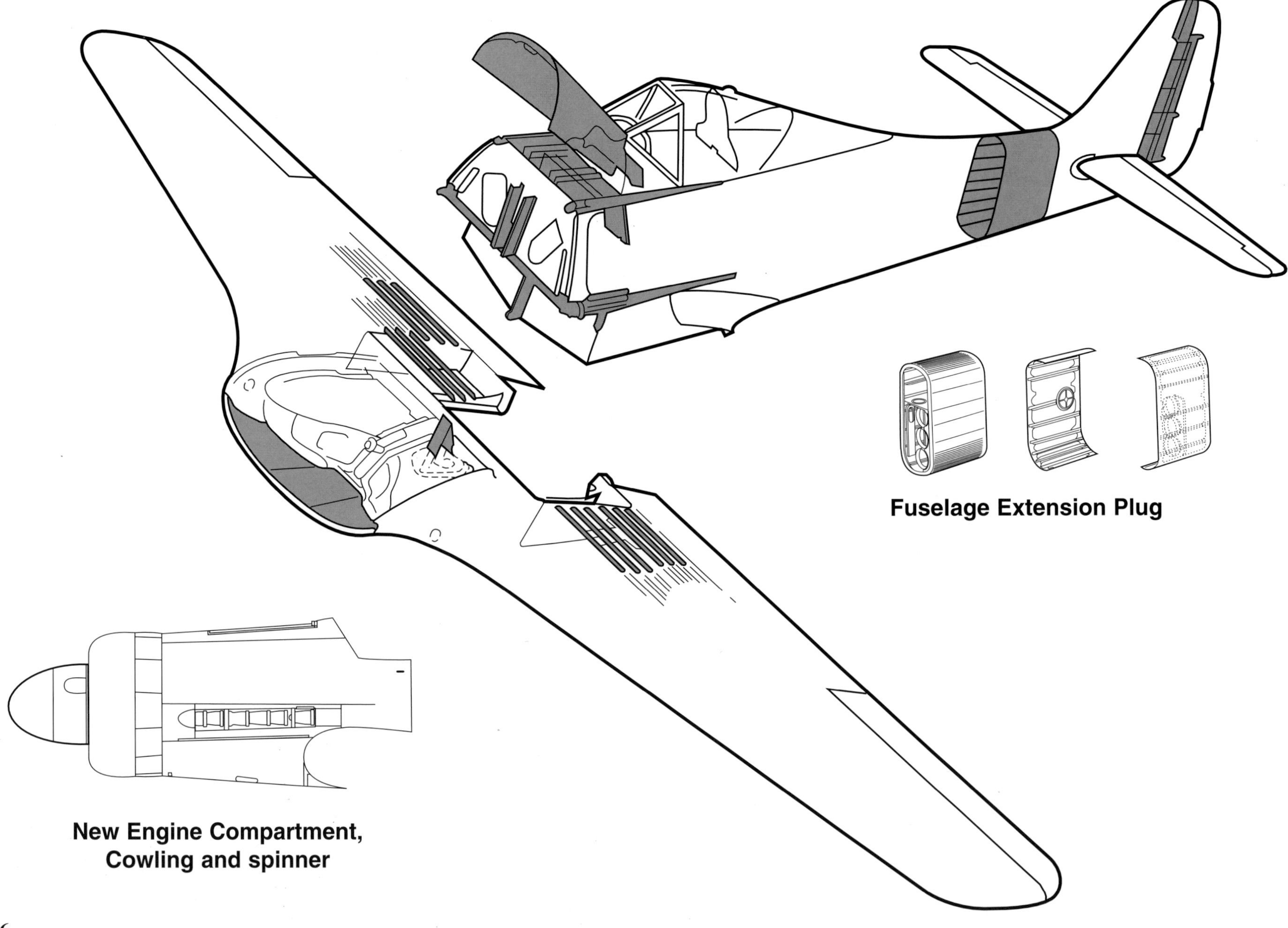

Fuselage Extension Plug

New Engine Compartment, Cowling and spinner

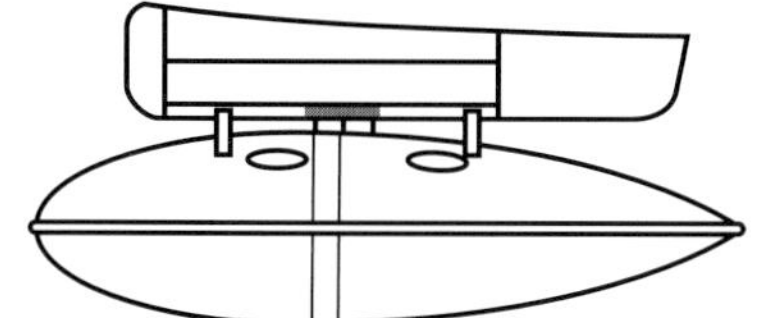

**ETC 504 Fusealge Rack
with 300 litre Tank**

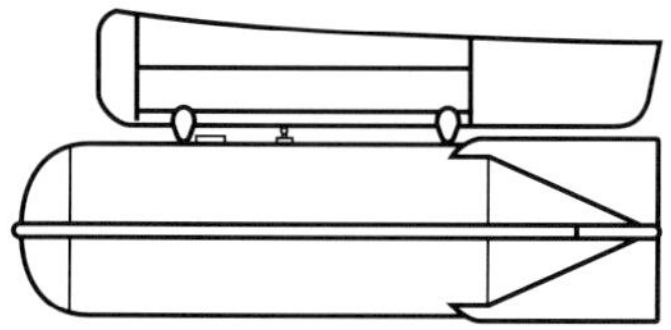

**ETC 504 Fuselage Rack
with AB 250 (250 kg) Bomb**

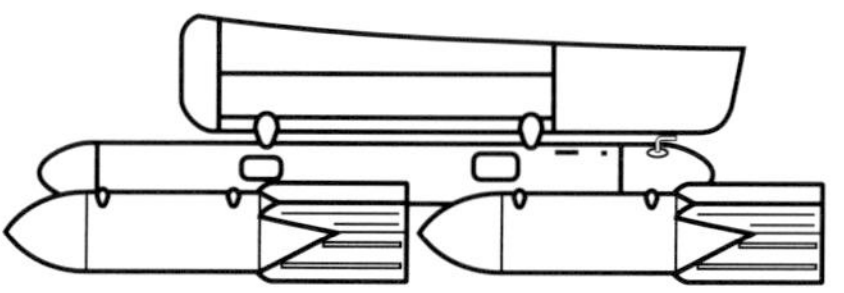

**ETC 504 Fuslage Rack with
ER-4 Rack with four 50kg Bombs**

ETC Wing Bomb Rack

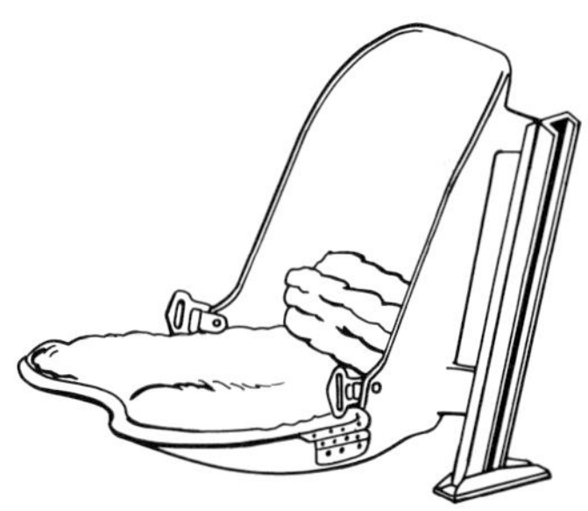

Pilot Seat

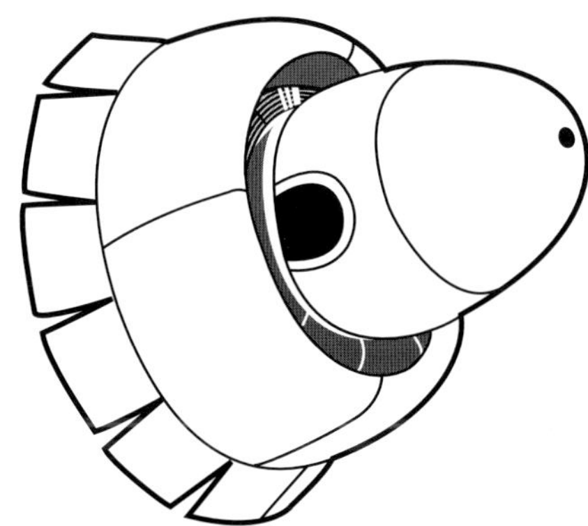

Extended Cowl Flaps

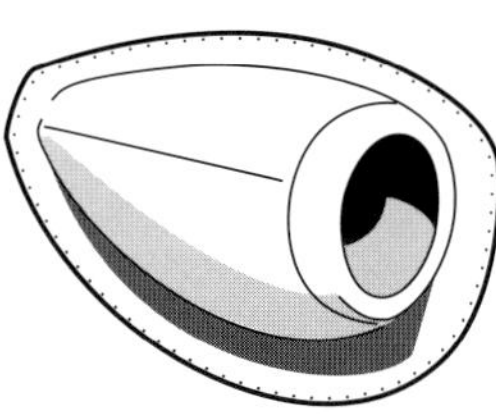

D-9 Air Scoop

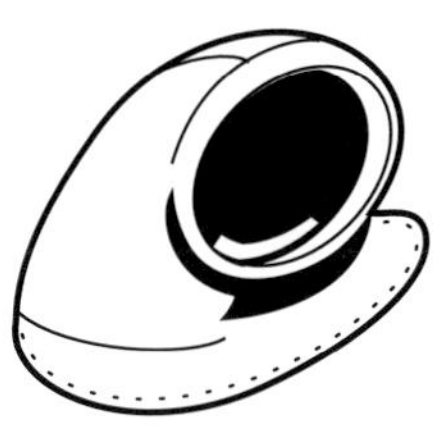

D-13 Air Scoop

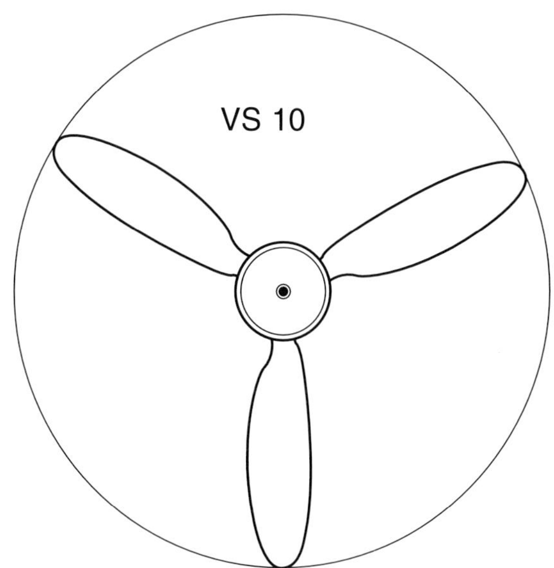

Propellers

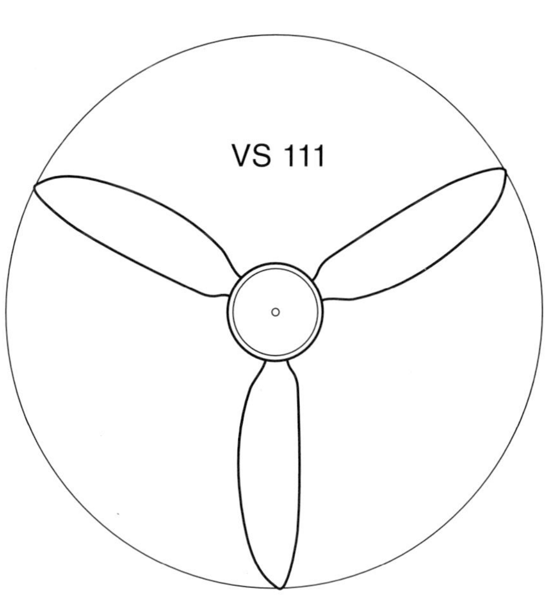

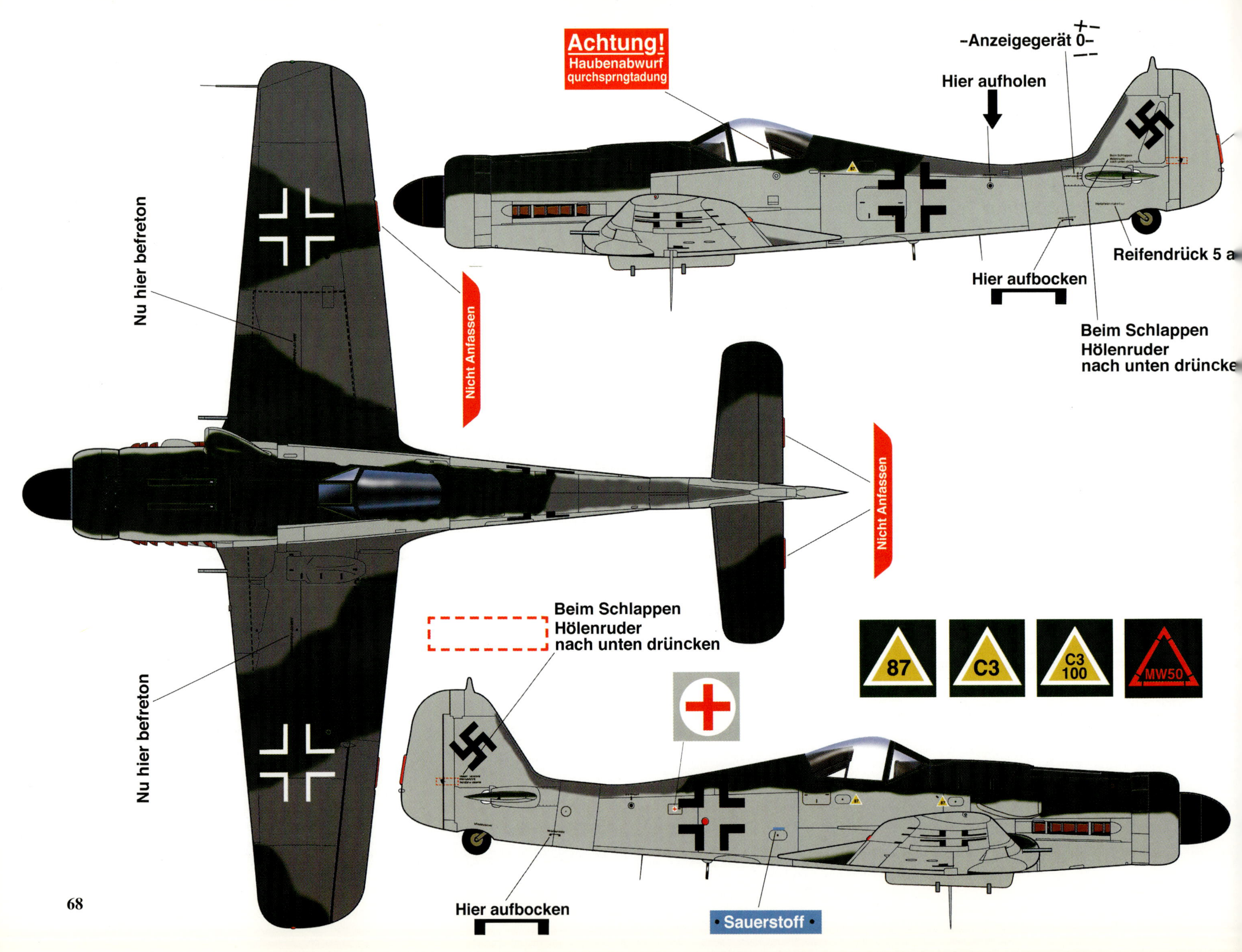

Achtung!
Haubenabwurf
qurchsprngtadung
-Anzeigegerät 0-
Hier aufholen
Nu hier befreton
Nicht Anfassen
Beim Schlappen
Hölenruder
nach unten drüncke
Reifendrück 5 a
Hier aufbocken
Nicht Anfassen
Beim Schlappen
Hölenruder
nach unten drüncken
Nu hier befreton
87
C3
C3
100
MW50
Hier aufbocken
Sauerstoff

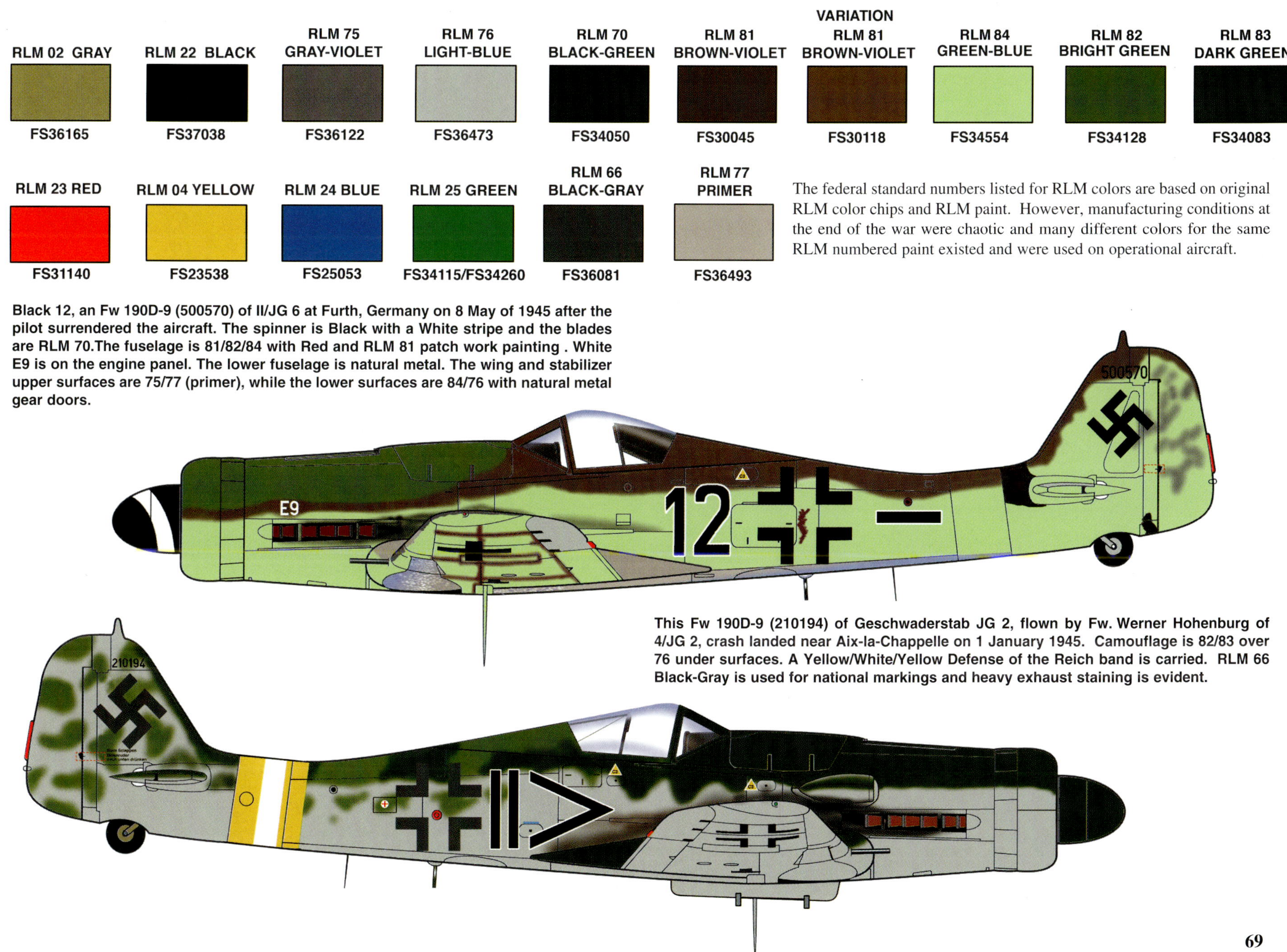

The federal standard numbers listed for RLM colors are based on original RLM color chips and RLM paint. However, manufacturing conditions at the end of the war were chaotic and many different colors for the same RLM numbered paint existed and were used on operational aircraft.

Black 12, an Fw 190D-9 (500570) of II/JG 6 at Furth, Germany on 8 May of 1945 after the pilot surrendered the aircraft. The spinner is Black with a White stripe and the blades are RLM 70.The fuselage is 81/82/84 with Red and RLM 81 patch work painting . White E9 is on the engine panel. The lower fuselage is natural metal. The wing and stabilizer upper surfaces are 75/77 (primer), while the lower surfaces are 84/76 with natural metal gear doors.

This Fw 190D-9 (210194) of Geschwaderstab JG 2, flown by Fw. Werner Hohenburg of 4/JG 2, crash landed near Aix-la-Chappelle on 1 January 1945. Camouflage is 82/83 over 76 under surfaces. A Yellow/White/Yellow Defense of the Reich band is carried. RLM 66 Black-Gray is used for national markings and heavy exhaust staining is evident.

Black 12 (W.Nr. 500570), an Fw 190D-9 of II/JG 6 at Furth, Germany. The pilot is shown surrendering the aircraft on 8 May 1945. The aircraft quickly became the subject that GIs wanted thier pictures taken with to send home. (J. V. Crow and D. Caldwell via Laing)

Blue 1 and 2, Fw 190D-9's of IV/JG 3 at Prenzlau in March of 1945. Blue 1 is believed to be Oberleutnant Oscar Romm's aircraft. Blue 2 has had its previous fuselage markings, possibly < - + - and a Defense of the Reich band, over painted. The aircraft at the far left may be an Fw 190D-11 or possibly a D-13. (D. Caldwell via Laing)

(Above and Below) Black <• + - (W.Nr. 211934), an Fw 190D-9 belonging to the Geschwader Technical Officer of (Stab)II/JG 6. Photographed at Furth, Germany, in May of 1945. Close examination of the aircraft reveal previous fuselage markings having been painted out under the <. (J. V. Crow)

(Above and below) Black 8 (W.Nr. 500581) an Fw 190D-9 of II/JG 6 at Halle, Germany. The aft latch on cowling gun panel is open throwing a shadow onto the fuselage. Several of the cloth covers over the bolts on the port landing gear cover have not been installed, although some repair work or re-paint has been performed on the cover. (J. V. Crow)

(Below)The tail has a great deal of mud splattered all over both the vertical and horizontal stabilizers that would indicate that the aircraft has operated from some very muddy airfields. (J. V. Crow)

Blue 1, an Fw 190D-9 of IV/JG 3 at Prenzlau during the spring of 1945. The aircraft appears to be an early production D series out of the Langenhagen factory with a two piece cowling gun panel. The spinner and propeller blades are Black. The fuselage is 83/75/76 with 02 mottled on the spine. The Canopy is 75/83. The tail has been spotted with 81. The fuselage extension plug is a band of 76, and the wing fillet bolts are painted 75. The wings and stabilizer are 83/75.

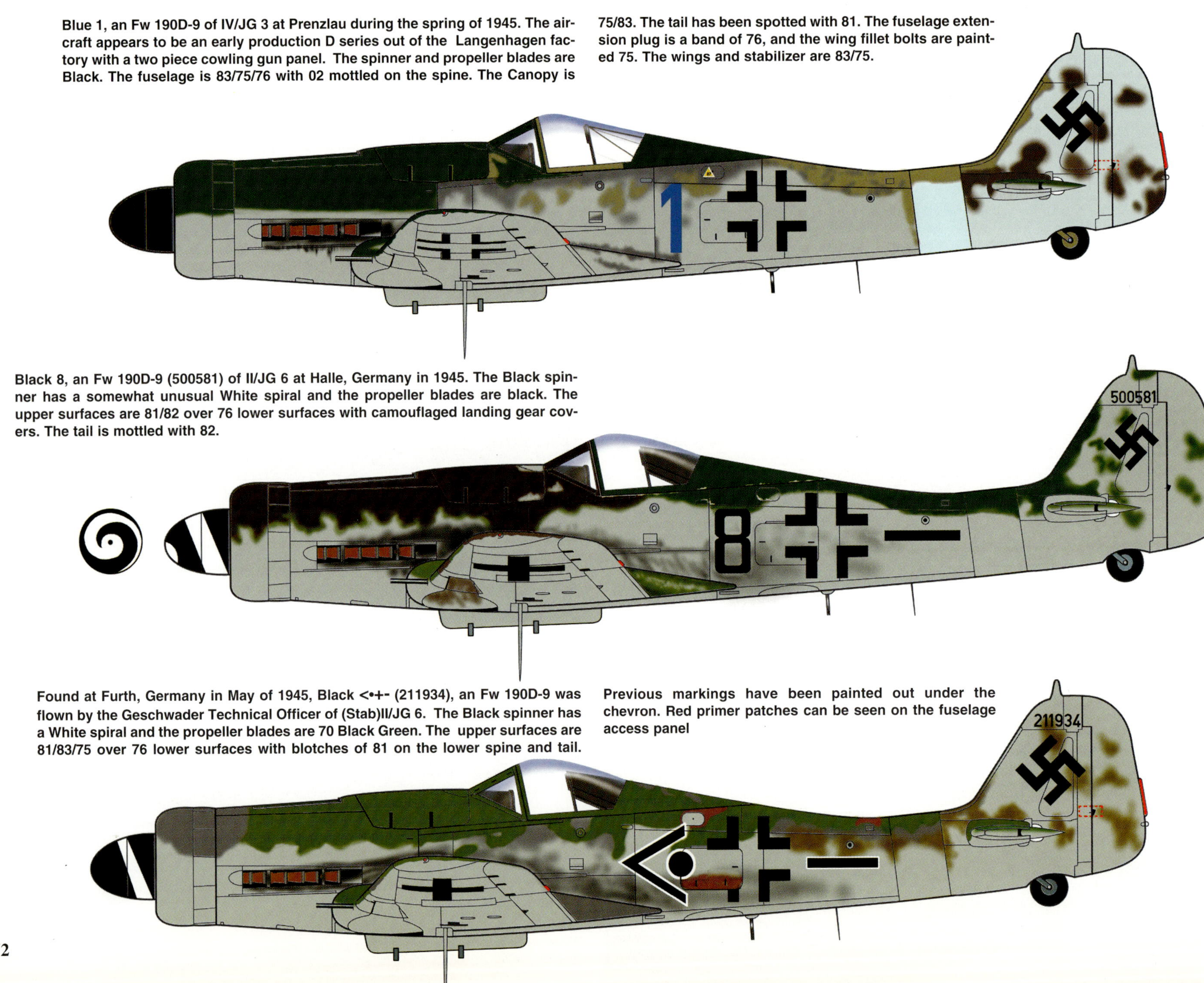

Black 8, an Fw 190D-9 (500581) of II/JG 6 at Halle, Germany in 1945. The Black spinner has a somewhat unusual White spiral and the propeller blades are black. The upper surfaces are 81/82 over 76 lower surfaces with camouflaged landing gear covers. The tail is mottled with 82.

Found at Furth, Germany in May of 1945, Black <•+- (211934), an Fw 190D-9 was flown by the Geschwader Technical Officer of (Stab)II/JG 6. The Black spinner has a White spiral and the propeller blades are 70 Black Green. The upper surfaces are 81/83/75 over 76 lower surfaces with blotches of 81 on the lower spine and tail. Previous markings have been painted out under the chevron. Red primer patches can be seen on the fuselage access panel

Double White chevron (the Work Number is listed as 220009, but is possibly 220005), an Fw 190D-11 at Bad Worishofen, Germany during the summer of 1945. The spinner and propeller are 70 Black Green. The fuselage is 83/75/76 with the fuselage extension plug partially in natural metal. The Upper wings and stabilizer are 83/75. The wing bottom is 76 with the leading edge and some under panels in natural metal.

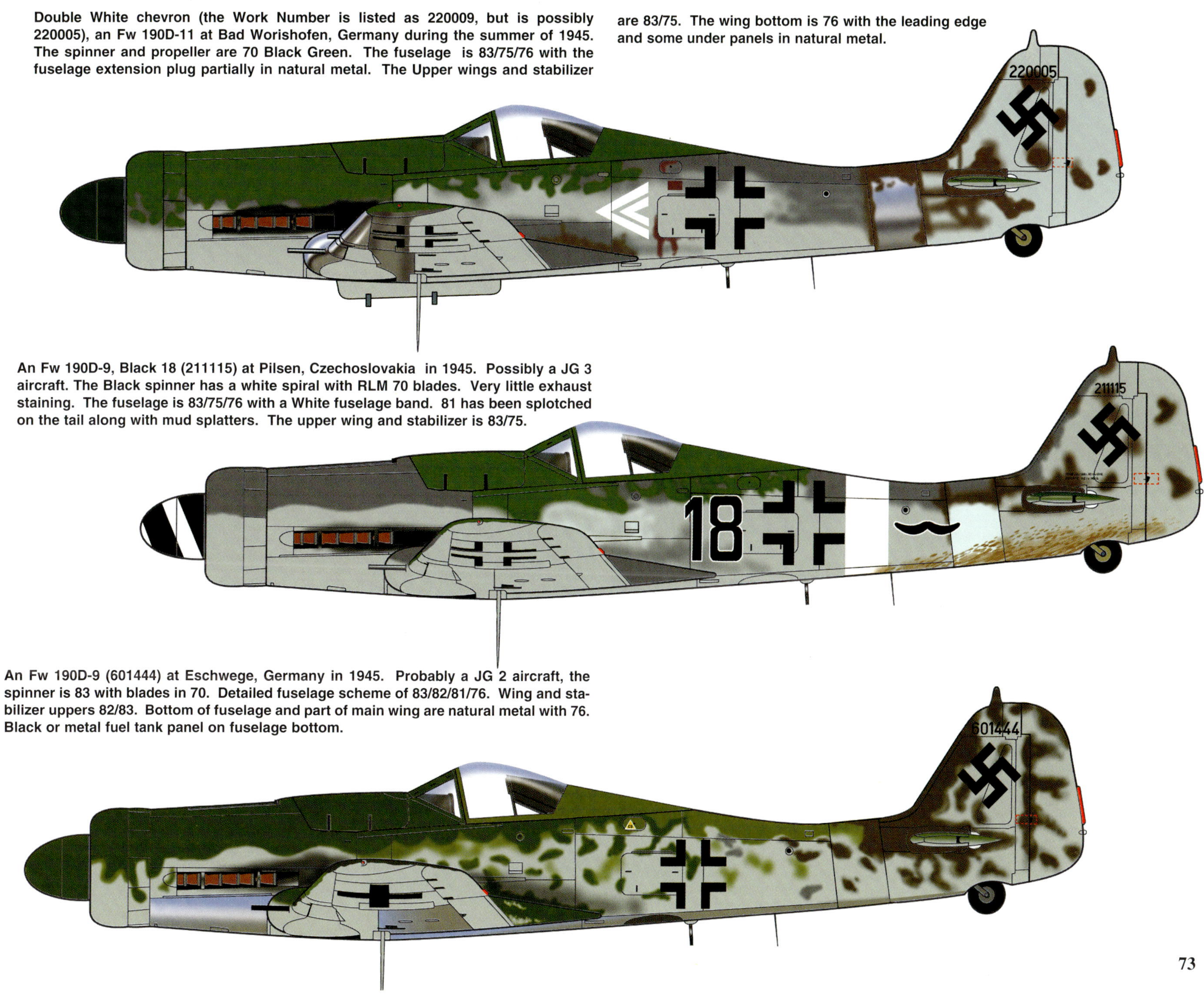

An Fw 190D-9, Black 18 (211115) at Pilsen, Czechoslovakia in 1945. Possibly a JG 3 aircraft. The Black spinner has a white spiral with RLM 70 blades. Very little exhaust staining. The fuselage is 83/75/76 with a White fuselage band. 81 has been splotched on the tail along with mud splatters. The upper wing and stabilizer is 83/75.

An Fw 190D-9 (601444) at Eschwege, Germany in 1945. Probably a JG 2 aircraft, the spinner is 83 with blades in 70. Detailed fuselage scheme of 83/82/81/76. Wing and stabilizer uppers 82/83. Bottom of fuselage and part of main wing are natural metal with 76. Black or metal fuel tank panel on fuselage bottom.

This Fw 190D-9 (W. Nr.211041) carries the Black Double Chevrons of a Gruppen Kommandeur. Photographed at Bayreuth-Bindlach during the summer of 1945 after Germany's capitulation. (J. V. Crow)

This Fw 190D-9 (W.Nr. 601444) at Eschwege, Germany in 1945 is believed to be an aircraft of JG 2. The paint on the fuselage sides is very distinctly mottled, but without any markings other than the somewhat smaller than usual black cross. The bottom of the aircraft and part of the main wing appears to be natural metal. (J. V. Crow)

With little thought to salvage Black double chevron, along with many other aircraft were bulldozed into pits and burned. This series of photographs depicts what happened to the thousands of aircraft at the end of the war. (J. V. Crow)

(Above and below) Black 18, an Fw 190D-9 (W.Nr. 211115) at Pilsen, Czechoslovakia in 1945, is believed to be an aircraft of JG 3. The machine has the port fuselage access panel removed as well as the radio access panel on the starboard side. Under the fuselage/wing center the 20mm ammo bay door is open and hanging down. (J. V. Crow)

(Above) White << (W.Nr. 220005 or W.Nr. 220009), an Fw 190D-11 at Bad Worishofen was a high ranking officer's aircraft possibly from the Stab General der Jagdflieger. The long, flat cowling is very evident as well as the different color of the fuselage plug (heavily painted on its upper surface) added to the re-built Fw 190A fuselage for the Fw 190D fuselage configuration. (Petrick via Wadman)

 Black 10 (W.Nr. 500613), an Fw 190D-9 of III/JG 26 found at Celle, Germany. 'USA 15' and a star in white has over painted the fuselage cross position. This Work Number was not listed as being returned to the US and the fate of the aircraft is not known. (J. V. Crow)

An Fw 190D-9 with a pair of ETC bomb racks under each wing. Not all Fw 190Ds were used as fighters, many became ground attack aircraft. The FW 190D was capable of carrying either two ETC 50 or ETC 71 bomb racks under each wing as well as an ETC 504 fuselage centerline rack. (J. V. Crow)

Yellow 10 (W.Nr. 836017), an Fw 190D-13 of I/JG 26. Surrendered at Flensburg, it is now on display at the Champlin Fighter Museum. The small JG 53 *Pik As* (Ace of Spades) emblem can almost be seen under the cockpit just above the leading edge of the wing. (J. Ethell via Laing)

White 16, an Fw 190D-9 (W.Nr. 500636), at Bayreuth-Bindlach, during the summer of 1945. The aircraft appears to have had the wing root 20mm cannon panel and the wing root fillet bolts painted with a much darker color than the surrounding panels. The Fw 190 to the right of white 16 has much the same in that the wing fillet is either unpainted or painted RLM 76 with dark painted attaching bolts. (J. V. Crow)

White 16, an Fw 190D-9 (500636) at Bayreuth-Blindlach, Germany during the summer of 1945. The spinner is Black with a white spiral and 70 blades. The fuselage is 83/75/76. The wing fillet is 75. The attachment bolts for the wing root cannon panel and wing root fillet are much darker than panels. The tail assembly is heavily painted with 83/75/76. The upper wing and stabilizer is 83/75.

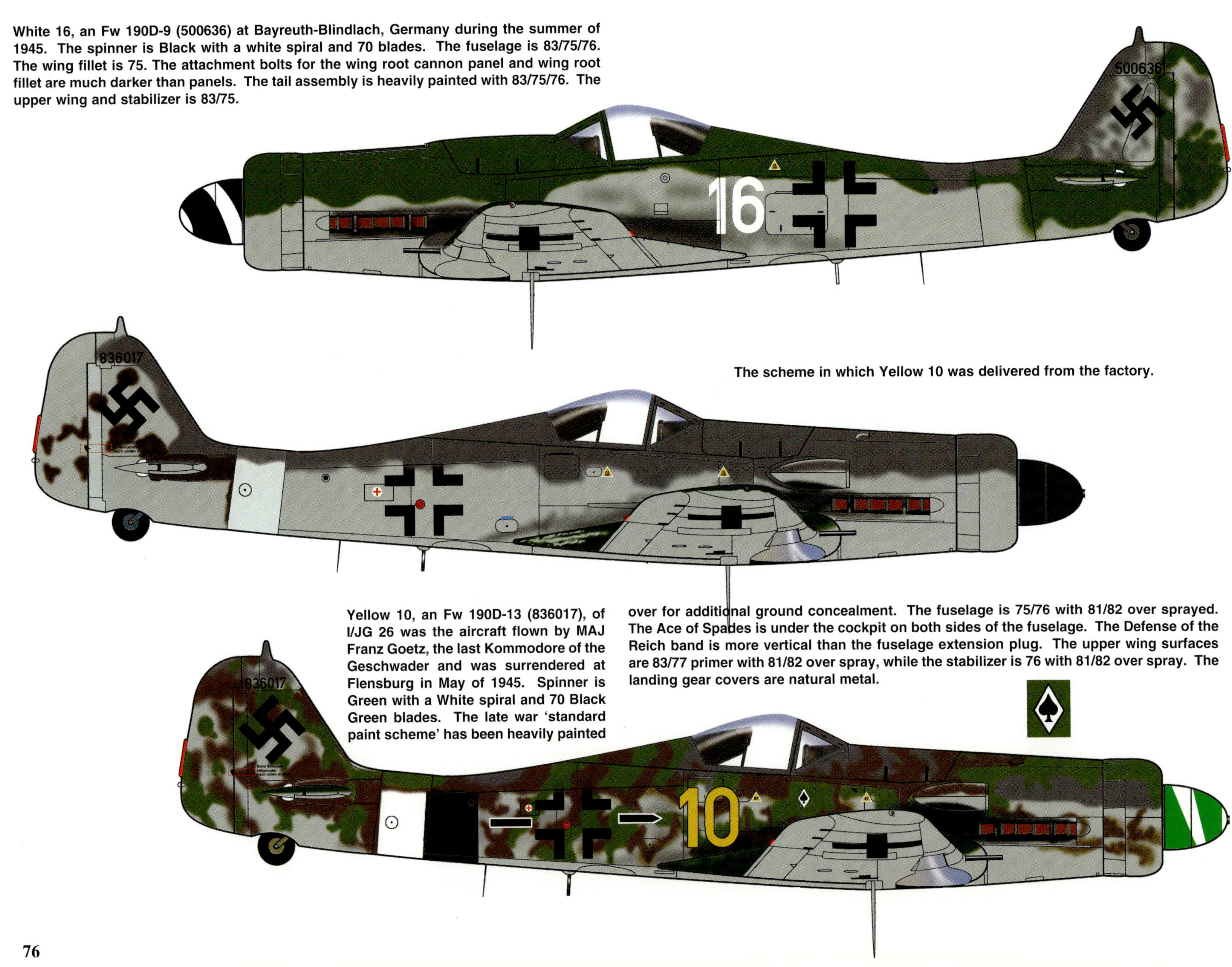

The scheme in which Yellow 10 was delivered from the factory.

Yellow 10, an Fw 190D-13 (836017), of I/JG 26 was the aircraft flown by MAJ Franz Goetz, the last Kommodore of the Geschwader and was surrendered at Flensburg in May of 1945. Spinner is Green with a White spiral and 70 Black Green blades. The late war 'standard paint scheme' has been heavily painted over for additional ground concealment. The fuselage is 75/76 with 81/82 over sprayed. The Ace of Spades is under the cockpit on both sides of the fuselage. The Defense of the Reich band is more vertical than the fuselage extension plug. The upper wing surfaces are 83/77 primer with 81/82 over spray, while the stabilizer is 76 with 81/82 over spray. The landing gear covers are natural metal.

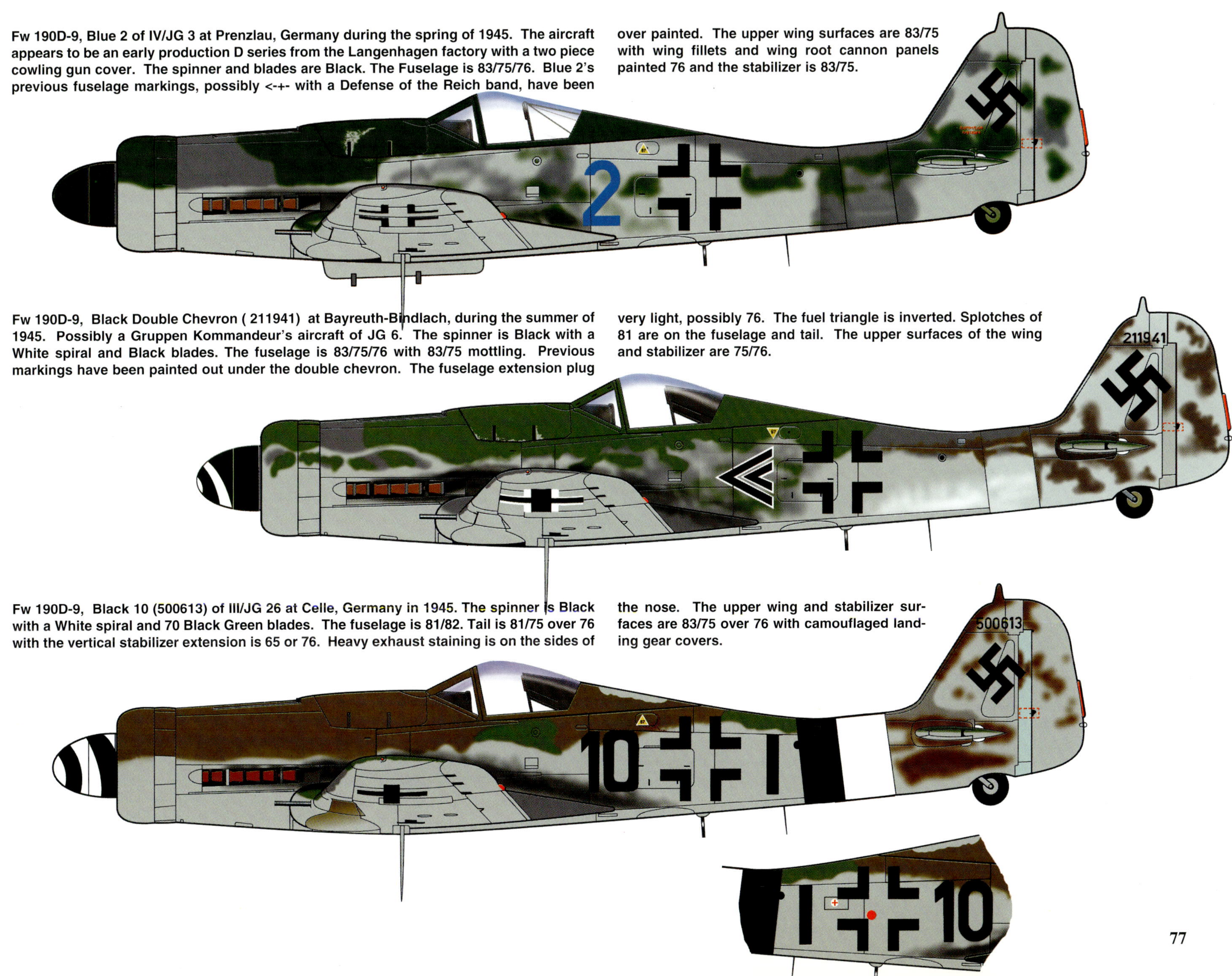

Fw 190D-9, Blue 2 of IV/JG 3 at Prenzlau, Germany during the spring of 1945. The aircraft appears to be an early production D series from the Langenhagen factory with a two piece cowling gun cover. The spinner and blades are Black. The Fuselage is 83/75/76. Blue 2's previous fuselage markings, possibly <-+- with a Defense of the Reich band, have been over painted. The upper wing surfaces are 83/75 with wing fillets and wing root cannon panels painted 76 and the stabilizer is 83/75.

Fw 190D-9, Black Double Chevron (211941) at Bayreuth-Bindlach, during the summer of 1945. Possibly a Gruppen Kommandeur's aircraft of JG 6. The spinner is Black with a White spiral and Black blades. The fuselage is 83/75/76 with 83/75 mottling. Previous markings have been painted out under the double chevron. The fuselage extension plug very light, possibly 76. The fuel triangle is inverted. Splotches of 81 are on the fuselage and tail. The upper surfaces of the wing and stabilizer are 75/76.

Fw 190D-9, Black 10 (500613) of III/JG 26 at Celle, Germany in 1945. The spinner is Black with a White spiral and 70 Black Green blades. The fuselage is 81/82. Tail is 81/75 over 76 with the vertical stabilizer extension is 65 or 76. Heavy exhaust staining is on the sides of the nose. The upper wing and stabilizer surfaces are 83/75 over 76 with camouflaged landing gear covers.

White <61, (W.Nr.350158, but possibly W.Nr. 220004) an Fw 190D-11 at Bad Worishofen during the summer of 1945. The aircraft retains its spinner for the engine mounted cannon, but the cannon was not installed, however, the wing's 20mm inboard and 30mm outboard cannons are clearly seen as are the unusual leading edge aircraft numbers painted just outboard of the 20mm cannons. (Petrick via Wadman)

(Above) Red 1, an Fw 190D-9 (W.Nr. 600424), of JV 44's protection flight, the Würger-Staffel or Sachsenberg Schwarm, commonly mis-referenced as the Papagie Staffel. Based at Munchen-Riem in May of 1945, these piston engined aircraft were assigned the task of protecting the Me 262 jets from marauding allied fighters during take-offs and landings. Since the field was also heavily protected by flack batteries these airfield defense fighters had their lower surfaces brightly painted to be quickly recognized as friendly aircraft by the flack crews. The inscription on the fuselage translates: Sell my clothes I'm going to Heaven. (D. Wadman)

(Below) Red 1 showing the special Red paint and White recognition stripes applied to the aircraft's entire underside. The bottom paint and striping was applied 'in the field' and as such was far from perfect. (D. Wadmam)

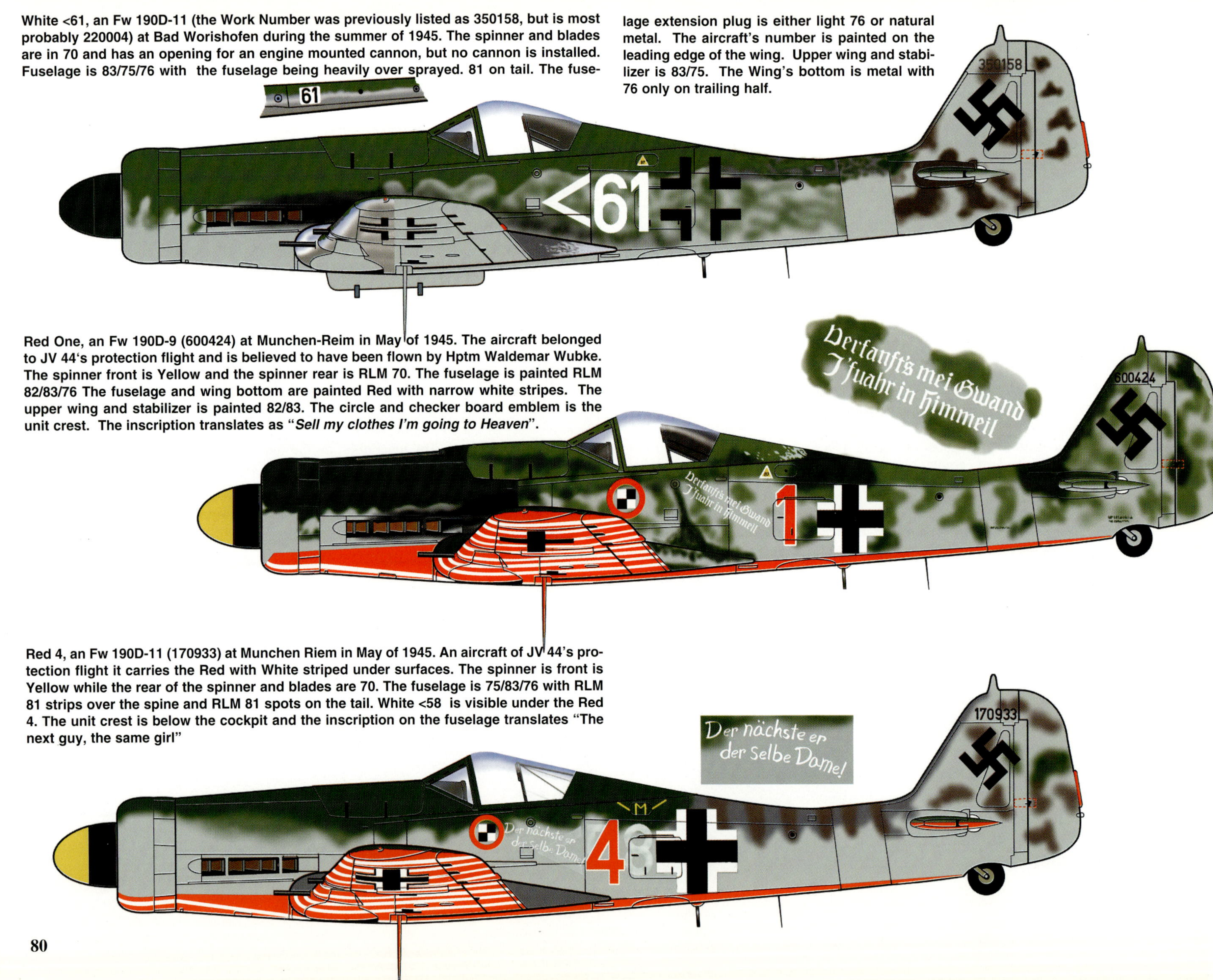

White <61, an Fw 190D-11 (the Work Number was previously listed as 350158, but is most probably 220004) at Bad Worishofen during the summer of 1945. The spinner and blades are in 70 and has an opening for an engine mounted cannon, but no cannon is installed. Fuselage is 83/75/76 with the fuselage being heavily over sprayed. 81 on tail. The fuse- lage extension plug is either light 76 or natural metal. The aircraft's number is painted on the leading edge of the wing. Upper wing and stabilizer is 83/75. The Wing's bottom is metal with 76 only on trailing half.

Red One, an Fw 190D-9 (600424) at Munchen-Reim in May of 1945. The aircraft belonged to JV 44's protection flight and is believed to have been flown by Hptm Waldemar Wubke. The spinner front is Yellow and the spinner rear is RLM 70. The fuselage is painted RLM 82/83/76 The fuselage and wing bottom are painted Red with narrow white stripes. The upper wing and stabilizer is painted 82/83. The circle and checker board emblem is the unit crest. The inscription translates as "*Sell my clothes I'm going to Heaven*".

Red 4, an Fw 190D-11 (170933) at Munchen Riem in May of 1945. An aircraft of JV 44's pro- tection flight it carries the Red with White striped under surfaces. The spinner is front is Yellow while the rear of the spinner and blades are 70. The fuselage is 75/83/76 with RLM 81 strips over the spine and RLM 81 spots on the tail. White <58 is visible under the Red 4. The unit crest is below the cockpit and the inscription on the fuselage translates "The next guy, the same girl"